KICK ROCKS: THE BOOK

Be Real. Be Free. Be You.

Chase Murphy, Jr.

What do you want?

You, beautiful you.

Whatever happens, I promise you, it is real and it is founded on the truth that LOVE, true love, the whole of love, is who we really are.

And there is that word... Love.
What does it mean?
What has it wrought?
What has it cost?

For those of you that know, we "know".

That very thing we sought the most and yearned to feel and know, and have, and live, and be protected by, and call our own, is the very thing that betrayed us.

That left us.

That abandoned us.

We were wrong.

Love, the true Love, has always been with us.

For that is who we are.

The bravest. The grandest. The truest. The realest.

Us.

You and I.

There is no normal.

"Anything and everything, anyone and everyone that would oppose the whole and free expression of who you really are and what you truly desire to be and to have, must Kick Rocks." — Chase Murphy, Jr., Founder of Kick Rocks.

If you can close your eyes and imagine the darkest moments in your life...

If you can sit silently and imagine the longing that you had for peace and comfort amidst the dread and anguish of feeling unworthy of love...

If you can close your eyes and see, imagine, the hopelessness of "being"...

Then you already have the power to live the life that you truly desire to live.

Then you already have the power to express who you truly desire to be.

Imagine what it could really be....

"For as he thinketh in his heart, so is he..." (*King James Version*, Proverbs 23:7)

For most of my life I was too afraid to write this book. I was too afraid to acknowledge out loud, so that even I was able to hear it, that I was still wrapped up in the ideals of my parents and family when it came to loyalty. And even more, I was still wrapped up in the idea that what they thought of me defined who I really am; I was afraid of what they might think of me still. I was too afraid that I would hurt their feelings and make them feel wronged by my "speaking out". I didn't want to be cut off from the very people that I had relied upon to validate my existence; I believed that I needed their approval to live my life as I wanted to live it. And even though I rationally and logically knew that I was free, there was still that lingering tendril of doubt.

Truth and honesty were to have been the tenets I was taught to embrace and live by. And yet, those very processes and tenets were also the stumbling blocks to my full and complete freedom from a past not wholly of my own making. In so many ways, to and for so many of us, we can talk about honesty and truth and yet, we are still unable to truly embrace it because if we do, there is knowledge that we will have to face the secrets that we carry, relive the trauma and more, have to contend with how we really feel more about ourselves than others. We can debate the truths. We can speculate about truths. We can question them. And in so many ways, I think that we do talk, debate, speculate and question "truth and honesty". Perhaps you don't but, for many of us, myself included, we do; many of us question the truth and value of honesty in our everyday lives.

So with that in mind, I am going to share my whole "truth" in this "opening" as it relates to this book.

Even as I write this, there are parts of me that want to edit this thing to within a semicolon of its life to make sure that it might make sense and yet, bypass some of the darker aspects of why I had to write this book. As contradictory as this may seem, this is a truth that most of us have to acknowledge every moment of every day; how much of the truth do I have to acknowledge knowing that it may cause "harm" to another? For me, as a writer, I also know that I do such heavy editing and second-guessing because I never seem to feel satisfied with the end result. And because of that, for years, many things didn't get completed because I expected perfection from myself; I was driven to meet expectations for life that I hadn't even created for myself. But you know, for those of us that spend our lives trying to outrun our sense of perfectionism or unworthiness, no matter what I, we, write, or do, it seemingly won't ever be enough. It won't ever be good enough. It will never satisfy. We will beat "it", that ever-elusive sense of completed perfection, literally, to death. We will critique it, spin it, rewrite it, burn it, piss on it and then cry over how we wish we could have truly expressed what it was/is that we felt/feel.

So, what the fuck am I talking about?

I wrote this book that I hoped would change the lives of those that have been physically, emotionally and sexually abused. I thought that my history, my experiences and the things that I thought I "knew" would somehow inspire others to live and love. I believe that my experiences and the resulting truths I have come to know could, and would, assist you to get beyond whatever limitations you find yourself beholden to.

I *believe* with all I am, that we are not broken.

That we have never really been broken.

And no one can ever break us!

Yes, that is what I believe.

That is what I live.

But with this book, I had it all outlined, spell-checked, edited and critiqued by many - to the point where I believed that it was ready to be published. I did everything that some highly-rated blogs suggested that I do. I did everything that I was told was going to make the book better. I did. Even though I can be hardheaded and stubborn beyond even the most accepting patience in my own soul, I nevertheless did what was told to me because I trusted the "pros".

In the end, what I finally accepted was that this book is really nothing more than my journey about reaching a point in life where I can share with people, other than counselors and groups, that I was sexually abused, emotionally and physically abused to the point where I damn-near succeeded in taking my own life; I just plain ol' didn't give a fuck about this bullshit process that people kept calling "life" to which I was to have been most thankful.

Fuck that. And them.

I just wanted to feel loved.

I guess, in truth, there really isn't a great set of steps in this writing designed to aid in anyone else's healing because I am not your yogi, guru or genie. In the end, I guess this is just a very public journal about some "Black" dude with tattoos that finally found reasons and the courage to live when others thought that I should die. Or be "dead".

And yet, I also know that for those that know what I am talking about, you will also know that I won't bullshit you, or blow smoke up your ass; I am here because I finally learned that I am *SO* worth being loved for just as the FUCK I am.

Right. The. Fuck. Now.

And so are you.

I wrote this book because I want you to live and love yourself for who the fuck you are right now. For yourself, and not any other breathing person on this earth. For you. For. You. You have earned it. I promise you. You have. You may not know and you may not believe it but, you have earned the right to Be You.

Whatever the title of this book may have meant to you, and whatever inspired you to consider it, I want you to know that it was written by a man that has no ulterior motives other than to see you find a place in your life where you can, and do, rejoice at being you;

I'm putting it right out there from the beginning.

I wrote this book because so few people had the courage to tell me during most of my life, what I have now come to know as the truth. This isn't to suggest that they lied, or had evil intent. Rather, I now believe that they simply didn't know what the real truth was. A truth that didn't fit the norm, or the expectations foisted upon me because "that's the way it's always been" or because "that's the right thing to do".

Nope, not why I wrote this book.

I wrote this book because there was a time in my life, when I only wanted someone to tell me the whole truth. Not a convenient, palatable, easy-to-digest truth but, one that was, *the* truth.

I wanted to know why people seemed to find it so easy to shit on me on a regular basis, and more, why it was sometimes done with such a sense of ease that it left me feeling completely inconsequential. Why did I have to be the one that felt like shit? What was so wrong with me that I was "that person", the one that others sought out to torment?

I wanted to know why it was so easy, later in life, for me to consider suicide as the best way to end feeling the way that I did. I wanted to understand, I thought then, why it seemed that the people doing the shit to me were able to go about their business and lives, without so much as a backwards glance at me after what they'd done.

I wanted to know what I had to do to be worthy of being loved, truly loved, by the people that told me regularly that they loved me and yet, in my mind, seemed to do so much ugliness – all in the name of love. I wanted to be more than someone else's idea of what love was.

I wanted someone to love all of me. To love and cherish all the broken, odd, misshapen places and pieces that made me who I was.

I just wanted to be loved.

So, if your life is hunky-dory and moving along perfectly,

moving just as you want it to, I can tell you that this is not the book for you. I didn't write this for you.

I wrote this for those that think of themselves as "not perfect".

I wrote this book to share a truth that we are all magnificent, glorious and wholly lovable beings. But sometimes, we need to be reminded and more, to be shown how to express and live and love who we *really* are.

And that is what this book is all about.

One man, sharing with others, one way to finally love one's true self, just as we are, right now.

Dedication

You will know who you are. You will know, with every fiber of your being, for whom this is written.

For every moment that you've questioned your purpose on this earth, for you, I have written this. For every night that you have laid awake, stifling your tears, so that no one would hear, for you, I have written this.

For every moment that you've considered a life beyond this one, for you, I have written this.

For every "yes", when you wanted to say "no". For every question unanswered. For every glimpse in the mirror, and not knowing who it was you saw looking back. For each and every moment that you've longed to just, be, loved. Just loved.

Seen. To just really be seen. To know that being seen was good enough. That being heard, was okay. That a voice of kindness, a word of genuine encouragement, a peace to call our own, a sense of belonging to something gentle and loving, seemed always just out of reach; so close and yet still beyond our grasp.

I dedicate the entirety of this book to you, the seeker, the questioning few; knowing now, in this moment, that we are not alone.

You are my brothers and sisters. Every one of you.

And we are silent no more.

Chase Murphy, Jr.
Spring, 2016

To my wife.

"The secret of health for both mind and body is not to mourn for the past, nor to worry about the future, but to live the present moment wisely and earnestly." – Gautama Buddha

"If you are depressed, you are living in the past. If you are anxious, you are living in the future. If you are at peace, you are living in the present." – Lao Tzu

"Love endures with patience and serenity, love is kind and thoughtful, and is not jealous or envious; love does not brag and is not proud or arrogant. It is not rude; it is not self-seeking, it is not provoked [nor overly sensitive and easily angered]; it does not take into account a wrong endured. It does not rejoice at injustice, but rejoices with the truth [when right and truth prevail]. Love bears all things [regardless of what comes], believes all things [looking for the best in each one], hopes all things [remaining steadfast during difficult times], endures all things [without weakening]." – Amplified Bible, 1 Corinthians 13:4-7

"You can search throughout the entire universe for someone who is more deserving of your love and affection than you are yourself, and that person is not to be found anywhere. You yourself, as much as anybody in the entire universe, deserve your love and affection." – Gautama Buddha

"He who is without [any] sin among you, let him be the first to throw a stone at her." – Jesus

"A man cannot be comfortable without his own approval." – Mark Twain

"I have taken back, that which I thought to have been taken. I now see, that to which I had been blind. Now. Now. Now. I know what love is." – Chase Murphy, Jr.

Table of Contents

Before You Begin

You need a heads-up. Right here. Right now. As will clearly be expressed throughout this book, I am outspoken, honest, transparent and not terribly interested in trying to satisfy those people that think that they have all the answers. In fact, if you're reading this to dissect the text and examples for imperfections, well, I can save you some time. One, I don't profess to be perfect, so it stands to reason, that this book isn't perfect. But two, and more importantly, I'm fully aware that this book isn't for everyone, and because of that, I'm not trying to please everyone. This book is about taking the risks, and having the patience and courage, to find oneself and love the person that's discovered. It's about learning to accept and celebrate every ounce of who we've come to be, regardless, and in many ways, in spite of, what others may think or say to, or about us. And finally, in a world that seems intent on finding reasons to say negative things about others, I want it fully understood, that for the most part, I am generally immune to small-minded people that seek to harm others. In other words, bullies don't bother me anymore. So, if you're a bully, if you think that being negative is your way of being "real", I would personally suggest that you check out what it means to be "real". Being real has nothing to do with seeking out reasons to be cruel, or negative, or belittling. But hey, that's just my opinion and I respect your right to have yours.

So, if you want to be an asshole, be an asshole – that is most assuredly, your right. Just understand that, however much I respect your right to live as you choose, that doesn't give you the right to impose your worldview on mine, or the lives of others. That's what I have an issue with; people who seem to think that their right to have an opinion or thought, somehow gives them a right to impose those on others. *You have a right to be you, and yet, I have a right to be me, and that means free from your toxic, negative views and thoughts. And your thoughts of who I am, what I am worth, what I should do with my life, and on, and on, are entirely your thoughts, and you are free and welcome to have them. But in the end, just because you may see me one way, doesn't make it so. And it doesn't mean that I have to hear it.*

I am not a psychologist or a preacher/religious leader. I am a fifty-something year old private Life Coach but, even within that context, I'm a different kinda coach. This book deals openly and graphically with childhood sexual molestation and rape, as well as childhood physical abuse. Additionally, there is frequent and open discussion about suicide. If any of these matters and topics bother you, this is not the book for you. The language is adult, it is frank and it is, at times, graphic. I don't apologize or offer any substitutes for the life that I have lived and along with that, I respect you enough to let you know in advance that this is not always a "feel-good" experience. Finally, it is my belief that there are enough of us, perhaps even you, that are ready for people to stop glossing over things with pretty words and descriptions, clinical and scientific language to explain "comfortably" the steps and processes of our own personal hells.

This book is not intended to take the place of counseling or therapy. In fact, as far as I'm concerned, a willingness to explore positive avenues such as counseling for healing is encouraged. But make sure that you find a counselor that you trust, one that you can be honest with. One that has a heart for people, and not just fat, juicy paychecks. If you're a counselor, and that last little bit offended you, well, as far as I'm concerned, you're probably part of the reason that people avoid counseling.

I am not trying to convince anyone into thinking that the choices I've made in my life are the choices that others must make. Nor am I attempting to recruit anyone for anything, nor am I proselytizing for (or against) any one organization or people. What I share here, whether my own experiences, or conclusions drawn from those experiences, are uniquely my own and not intended to replace yours. In any way, shape or form. Just as I respect yours, I ask that you respect my life in the sense that my experiences don't have to mirror yours. What I share in this book, I own. And I share it because, sadly, I realized that I am not the only one.

If this book isn't for you, that's okay.

But for the rest of you, us, those of us that have lived through "their own" personal hells, and to and for any of you that believe yourself beyond help and hope, because of that hell, I beg to differ with you. I know of what I speak.

There is happiness to be lived.

Let's do this, you and I.

Together.

- *Journal Entry, Oct. 1994*

I told someone my story and she asked me why I hadn't fought back. She asked me how I could have put myself in that position. She asked me why I hadn't run. I had nothing else to say. Nothing. She didn't understand and I didn't have answers for her.

I hated the way she looked at me. I felt like shit. She looked at me like I had done something terrible to her, like I was the one who had done the shit.

It hurts. There is no one to talk to. I shouldn't have even told her. Should have kept my mouth shut. -

Shortly after that entry went into my journal, I would, on November 2nd, 1994, try to take my own life. Though I had been the one raped and molested, and though I had been the victim of a predator, those who I had trusted enough to tell what had happened to me, had made me feel as though I was the one that carried the stigma, the burden of being the one "messed-up". Somehow, I'd become the one that carried the stench of abuse and degradation, humiliation and self-hatred for something having been done to me. And in my mind, it felt like everyone knew – that everyone could see just how filthy I was on the inside. It hurt thinking about what others thought of me. How they looked at me. It hurt. I'd hurt for too long, and I was done feeling the way that I'd felt.

I read an article recently about the signs that someone shows when they're considering suicide. Though the article was quite informative and touched on some very good points, for me, it was a load of shit because to try and give hints or peeks into the hearts and minds of those that are considering suicide is to suggest that someone on the outside can prevent it from happening; if someone wants to die, they're going to die. And again, for me, and many like me, we don't send out signals; we quietly go into ourselves, and wrap our pain around our *own* hearts because in truth, for so many of us, that's all we believed we would ever know. Pain.

And because of that belief, there are no specific warnings for others to pick up on; we just want to stop hurting. Our wanting to stop hurting isn't about harming others, or even about considering the feelings of others. How ever selfish people want to think of suicide, they often forget that at the root of it all, is the utter and complete need to stop hurting. So in that sense, it is the ultimate in selfishness – to want to feel loved and whole, worthy and cherished, valued and needed. When we decided on suicide as the answer, we just, did it. We just wanted to stop hurting. So it's not about warning signs or signals.

The decision isn't about other people. It's not always about someone that's emotionally or mentally ill. It's not about cowardice. It's not about taking an "easy way out". It has everything to do with our own deep need to stop hurting. You see, what so many don't understand, is that in our own way, we *did* seek out help. We did seek out, in our own way, someone to trust, someone to help us. In our own way of thinking, we did everything that we thought we should, or could do. We spoke up, we tried to show others that we needed and wanted help.

But they didn't understand just how deeply the pain was set. They were unable to comprehend, or even imagine just how much pain we were really in. We learned to keep up appearances, while at the same time inwardly trying to breathe. So long as we "looked" okay on the outside, those around us tended to think that everything was fine.

But we weren't fine. And that's what this book is about.

Stopping the pain, and getting on with the living.

Preface

One of the most important reasons for me deciding to write this book, and the manner in which I chose to express my thoughts, feelings and ideas, is that, in many ways, we as Americans have a very hard time talking about the tough aspects of human life and the frailty to which we are all subject to. Men are taught to be men, whatever the hell that means, and in this confusion, errors are made, judgments about self-worth are distorted and worst of all, we don't really talk about the damage and the results of our unwillingness to stop and reevaluate if the ideas of masculinity are effective in helping men be the best that they can be. We refuse to discuss it because, for the most part, we want to convince ourselves that it's working. That somehow, in the face of all the evidence to the contrary, the suicides, the abusive husbands, the drunkards, the mid-life crises, seemingly random affairs and other assorted expressions of unhappiness, are some aberrations or, as so many want to say, "men just being men". I say, Bullshit.

Girls are given pink dresses and frilly hair-barrettes, and told stories about the princess that needs to be rescued by the knight on a white horse, in shiny armor. Girls are told that they need to be "lady-like", to affect a certain degree of deference to men, so that they can maintain their femininity. And frankly, who in the world decided that women need to be "less than" men to be considered a "real woman"? As much progress as we seem to have made, we still find that there is an imbalance for women between what they should and can aspire to, and what society says they ought to. A woman is still subject to cultural biases in determining what she can do with her own body or her life. Somehow, she has to weigh how she will be viewed by society against what she truly desires to be.

But that is why this book is written. Time to talk about who we are without all the hubbub and bullshit that so often passes for rational thought and discourse. In this case, for the purposes of this book, we get to dismiss a great deal of the "sage wisdom" of the ages, and consider, for ourselves, just who we want to be, and to whom we owe our dreams and aspirations.

This book was written, from the very beginning, with the idea that I was going to be in partnership with those that are hurting and/or looking for, searching for a kindred spirit that's been through the fire and willing to share their discoveries without judgments. But more than that, this is about sharing truth. No tributes to some far-off, distant, external entity to whom allegiance must be pledged. This entire book is about an honest appraisal of who I thought that I was, to the understanding and realization of who I truly am.

On the one hand, it was suggested to me that I keep this book a middle of the road, inspirational text that included feel-good quotes from famous people and less-than-threatening examples from my life. Examples and stories that weren't too offensive, that didn't cause the mainstream to cringe, or draw back with disgust. Further, it was also suggested that I write in sweet, glowing terms with "acceptable" language that wouldn't frighten away a large part of the population that otherwise, might be willing to read my book.

I chose not to listen. I made a conscious choice to write this book in a manner that would be as close to my essence as I am capable of doing. I wrote this book the way I believe, the way I talk, and the way I *feel*. This book is written in a way that, if you and I had a chance to sit down and talk, there'd be little difference between the language in this book, and the language in our conversation. Although I will confess now, though it's not about intentionally shocking people, I swear like a proverbial "sailor".

Kick Rocks then, as a book, as a philosophy, as a way of relating to life, is a celebration for all of us that are not necessarily "normal". I am not simply talking about a "mainstream" understanding of what normal is or is not rather, this whole book and Kick Rocks is about empowering you to Be Real, to Be Free. To Be You.

Kick Rocks, for me, is like dancing, deep within the soul, like no one is watching, and you're free to just, be. Kick Rocks is about getting to a place *where you know that anyone, and anything that would oppose your freedom to be who you are, can literally, KICK ROCKS, and you have the courage and strength to say it. Live it.*

Define and live your own normal. Or, as a good friend of mine once told me years ago, "...fuck the haters. 'Cause someone's always gonna have some shit to say 'bout you. So fuck them *and* their bitch-ass opinions." Perhaps not the most eloquent way to say it, but it nevertheless illustrates a very real point; *you are not likely to ever stop people from speaking or thinking ill of you,* so for me, I had to learn to let my own voice, my own thoughts about me, who I was/am, who I wanted to be, become the overriding voice and thoughts about me and my world. As hard it was, since no one had really taught me how to live freely and clearly defined by *me,* it took some time. But I eventually got it. And that's what this book is really all about. Getting and staying, truly free.

I am a sentimental man. I learned how to hide it. I got really good at keeping it hidden from others because it kept people from asking too many questions, or pointing fingers. Or laughing at me. I kept my gentleness to myself because, in the world that I inhabited, it was simply safer emotionally. I learned how to swallow my emotions (and keep my tears to myself) while I was watching a gooey, emotionally-touching television show or movie. As an aside, I don't like the terms and phrases like "man up", "drives like a girl", "acts Black/White...", "chick-flicks", or a whole list of narrow-minded socially accepted colloquialisms, as I find the terms, and the ideas behind them, insulting not only to the object of the phrase but, to anyone else that loves a good, well-written, emotionally-touching tear-jerker; such phrases and terms reduce everyone to objects. The terms themselves, and the inherent meanings behind it, seek to diminish the expression of emotions, and they try to codify the terms as being something acceptable and considered a cultural norm. Which, to me, is utter bullshit. A Christmas movie, or a particularly beautiful piece of music moves my soul, and there are times when I want to experience the emotions in its most honest and raw form; it's how most of us are built. I want to experience it all. And my expressions are my own and not subject to the opinions and norms of others.

Hearing someone sing from the depths of their soul, is another moment that validates the wonder that is life. My point is, I am naturally a gooey-centered person but, over the years, through my childhood and teen years, I learned how to protect myself as best I could. And though many times, my adversaries were bigger, stronger and held all the power, I learned how to hide in plain sight, which more often than not, kept me from the worst of the worst that I could have imagined. I learned, and nearly mastered, the art of soul-shrinkage – making myself as still and small inside and outside as possible.

Just to give you an idea of just how sentimental I am, and how much that sentimentality is a part of me, I'll share with you my first experience at being moved to tears in public.

I was in seventh grade, and it was a field trip to see a movie. For me, going to see a movie in a real theater was a first and more than that, it was going to be experienced with a group and with a group, I had imagined the fun that we were all going to have. But the movie that we were going to see was *Romeo and Juliet*, and I had no idea at the time, even as a teenager, how that movie was going to affect me. This version of the film, was the 1968 British-Italian romance film, directed and co-written by Franco Zeffirelli, and starred Leonard Whiting and Olivia Hussey as Romeo and Juliet.

I watched that movie in silent amazement. The music, the words, the acting – everything – completely captivated me. And though I didn't understand the Shakespearian iambic pentameter at the time, I understood the emotion of the scenes as they played themselves out on the great screen in front of me. Most of the students had gotten themselves into their own little groups, girls with girls, and the boys with the boys but, for me, I was sitting in the middle of the theater all by myself. To this day, I don't know why I was alone but, whatever the reasons had been, I was by myself to focus entirely on the movie. I will spare you the details of my sniffling throughout the movie until the death scene in the tomb. When that happened, I was undone. So there I was, keeping the secret of sexual rapes hidden, and watching, on the big screen, two people that loved one another so deeply that they'd been willing to forsake all things for the chance to live their lives together. I realize that I had been too young to understand the full import of the movie but, that doesn't change how hard I'd fought to let no one know that I was crying. I lowered my head, squeezed my eyes shut and had covered my mouth but, I couldn't shut out the music. The words. Romeo's pain. I could hear it all. And when Juliet rose to find her beloved dead….

When the movie had ended and the lights came up, I didn't realize how much of a mess I was until one of the boys had pointed at me and made a comment about the "snot" on my face. In that moment, like so many others, I resolved to never let that happen to me again. I would remember to keep my heart private so that people wouldn't point fingers at me and laugh. But what I didn't know then, that I celebrate now, is that a loving heart frees not only your own soul, but it touches other kindred spirits. Because as much as the boys laughed, there was one girl, one someone special whose eyes were as red as mine apparently had been, that had briefly touched my hand and given me a look of understanding. Where one had laughed, another had understood.

With that said, though I have come to freely express the whole of my being as a gentle soul, I am not, by any means, anyone's footstool. There is a freedom in the liberation of the soul, in that ability and willingness to shed the past and the stifling, internal and perpetual commentary in our minds, most often in the voice of those that did not hold our best interests at heart. I get to sing in the shower – loud. Get to dance in the rain, laugh with my whole self. Get to enjoy the sun, the clouds, the moon...

Too "mushy" for you? Well, it was not always this way. I did not always know the bounty of endless hope and the Soul-Salsa (for those of you that just read that, and thought, "what the hell is he talking about," I will address the Soul-Salsa in a later chapter) of laughter and hope; I get to enjoy butterflies in my belly just thinking about the way my wife smiles at me.

I wrote this book because children, some as young as eleven, which is not to suggest that this is the youngest by any stretch of the imagination, have come to the conclusion that death is the better alternative to living the life they were living. Eleven years old. Get your heart and mind around that. Eleven. But there is a frightening aspect of our American culture that wants to pretend that these suicides are not happening. Somehow, there is a belief that if it's not discussed, then it's not happening. Nevertheless, discussed openly or not, children are committing suicide at an alarming rate. Alarming? Yes, alarming; one death of a child over being bullied, humiliated and denigrated for being "different", or a "geek", or too small, too smart, too short, too "whatever-makes-them-unique" is one blessed death too many. So yes, alarming.

I want you to take a moment and get your mind and heart around that fact; a child, as young as eleven commits suicide because they don't want to be here on earth any longer. How does a child, a *child*, come to believe that suicide is an answer to any issues or problems that they may be facing? Think on that. Let that seep in. Close your eyes and try to imagine how shitty they must have thought their life to be, to decide to end their short existence on this earth. How desperate must they have been for love, for acceptance, for a place of peace that would have welcomed them to a new view and expression of life that allowed them expression of their truest self? How alone must they have felt to make the choice of finality over continuing to merely exist? These children chose death. Think on it. See it in your mind's eye.

I wrote this book because there is a darkness on this earth that is so often not talked about. And even when it is discussed, it's discussed in rational, clinical terms that for many of us, don't even begin to express the fullness of what we're feeling deep inside. This is not to say that professional counseling and therapy are not good ideas. In fact, I've had my share of counseling. But this book is not about demonizing or discarding counseling, nor is it intended to be a replacement for counseling. What my hope is, is that this book might serve as an inspiration for others to live. But not just "live", but to be happy. To have the joy that we all truly deserve.

This book is intended for folks that feel like something is off. That somehow, no matter how funny we may be, how witty and urbane our personalities appear on the outside, on the inside, we know that something is not quite as it should be. For the most part, there is not anything about us outwardly that others see, that would give any indication of just how sad, angry, lonely and lost we feel on the inside.

I wrote this book because I was asked to. Parents in my Life Coaching sessions asked me to share my story for others to read. They asked me to share my story in hopes that other children and parents might find a way to prevent others from believing that suicide is the *only* answer. They asked me to be brutally honest, to tell a truth that so many on the outside of the pains and darkness of suicide are unaware of, and more, to talk straight. We're trying to do more than just save lives here. We want to inspire hope in the face of the seemingly impossible lack of choices to remain here on this earth. We want people to believe, if at all possible, that life can be such a pleasure to experience.

And yet, sadly, I can already hear the voices of those that would say, "but you don't know what I've been through," and they would be absolutely correct. But I respond to those individuals with the following; you don't know me either but, if you give us, you and I, just a little time, there's no telling what we might discover. Together. Why? Because I care. Because I give a shit. Yes, I do. Really, I do.

I give a shit because I can relate. I care because there was a time when someone took the time to show me a compassion and understanding that I'd never experienced before, at the perfect time in my life, and this compassion and nonjudgmental willingness to share their experiences, may have been the one thing that literally saved my life. Because someone cared about me, at a time when I needed it most, it fills my heart to share, to open myself to those that are willing to hear, and at the very least, give me the benefit of the doubt when I say, "I care about you," whether you can believe it or not, because that's how I'm built. Don't believe me? Well, what do you have to lose by reading these few pages? You never know what we might discover together. And even if, at the end, you think that this has all been a waste of your time, I will still care about you and what happens to you. It's just how I am, and you don't get to decide that for me. That's our partnership. I won't bullshit you. Ever.

I will say something right now, that few others are willing to say; I am not, in any way, shape or form, the solution to your problems, challenges or woes. I am not a savior. The happiness that you will come to experience will be of your own doing. Meaning, you don't owe me the credit. You won't be beholden to me as the one that "set you free". At best, I am merely a guide. A guide in the sense that I am willing to openly share my experiences with you and in that, I'll answer your questions in hopes of giving you information from which you can make your own decisions about what is best for you, and how you want to celebrate your life.

It is my personal belief that there are too many books and authors that want to lay claim to having a one-size fits all solution to your concerns. For example, though I am not opposed to prayer, I also don't believe that prayer alone will suffice in granting us the life that we truly desire. At best, it *seems* that prayer is a hit or miss proposition and at worst, it causes us to look outside of ourselves for assistance from a god that is too often portrayed as selective in regards to whose prayers do or don't get answered. This isn't to suggest that there is *no* god, rather, I am suggesting that when prayer is used as the only option, when there are other more expedient and appropriate avenues to accomplish and embrace that which we desire, we tend to find ourselves wondering why those prayers weren't answered. There are thousands of men and women that prayed for their children, only to later find themselves at their children's funerals asking, *"why..."?* But, if the notion of traditional, religion-based prayer works for you, I have all the respect in the world for that, *for you.* For the rest of us, and those that seek and need something either in addition to, or in place of prayer alone, we band together to share the pathways, processes and purposes that have granted us peace and happiness.

If this upsets you, I can assure you, I completely understand. Several years ago, there was no way that you could have convinced me that prayer doesn't work. Though I didn't have any real concrete evidence to support this claim, I nevertheless clung to those beliefs that had been instilled in me during my childhood, in spite of evidence to the contrary. But again, this is not about saying that prayer doesn't work. What I am saying, quite bluntly in fact, is that there is more that must be done than just prayer as the only avenue.

But why me? Why was I asked to write a book? And more, why should you read it? Bearing in mind that I'm no Ph.D., or a physician, or a religious leader, what could I possibly have to say that might benefit you? I have no academic credentials that would convince the world, or you, of how smart and talented I am. I have no professional association to which I belong, nor do I have a pedigree that distinguishes my aptitude or skill at addressing such critical issues as suicide prevention, intervention or counseling. In fact, on paper, with my DUI's, arrests, divorces, drinking issues, unemployment, a felony conviction for child support arrearage, children I have that I have no relationship with, it would appear that I am the least likely person to have anything to do with inspiring others, unless of course, on paper, you consider my history a cautionary tale.

On paper, and let's just say it as it is, *on paper*, I'm a fuck-up. On paper, I'm unemployable, at least in a job that pays a stitch above minimum wage. On paper, coupled with a background check, even a cursory one, the "facts" seem to cause employers to run away in droves. Here's a fact, even a well-known fast-food burger joint passed on me. I guess they don't want felons influencing your choice to upsize your combo-meal. Or maybe they are concerned that I might abscond with some pocket change and a bag of fries. But child support arrearage or not, it's a felony. And once you have the felony on your record, you enter into a world of dismay and veritable hopelessness, that's so deep and real, it nearly chokes the dreams out of you. Oddly enough, this is not about whining or crying rather, it's a testament to how our choices have very real consequences. The "facts", as they are, are pieces of information that, no matter how accurate, in no way give a full picture of the man that I am. But a part of the process of healing is not only to acknowledge one's past, but to accept it.

This acceptance does not excuse, nor does it justify the behavior however, so long as we continue to pretend or deny what has been done, we remain prisoners to the past. More on this later.

So why is this Black man talking about hope, inspiration and the too-often lost desires to live? Who the hell am I?

I love my parents. I wish them the greatest of life's blessings. I wish them all the joy that this universe has to give. But growing up, my parents were bullies, tyrants, abusive emotionally and psychologically, and more, physically. And I say this now, after all these years, because I have been able to define such treatment as behaviors exhibited by bullies and tyrants. For all of his warmth and kindness, my father's temper meant that he was quick with the weapons of his discipline from belts, an electrical extension cord, a rubber paddle or even, his hands. My father believed that to beat a child (which he called a "spanking") was to instill and apply discipline. To my father, a solid ass-kicking was the way to get a child as rambunctious and head-strong as I, to behave and do what he believed was the correct and right thing to do. I would guess that my parents would disagree with my version of the truth, and that's okay with me. But learning and living within the parental context, was not the only challenge that I would encounter to set my self-worth sideways.

When I was thirteen, the next-door neighbor decided that my ass was quite tempting, and as a result, I became his sexual plaything. This wasn't a one-time occurrence. I was introduced to sodomy up close and personal - over and over, and over. And over again, for nearly a year, give or take a few weeks. There's a pain to anal rape that is beyond description. And what I mean by that is, I really don't have the words to describe it. Learning how to hide bloody underwear from your mother is not something that any child should have to try and figure out. Ever. Having to swallow a grown man's cock, when you're a small thirteen-year-old child, is not something that should be on anyone's resume. But here's a truth that few people want to acknowledge, let alone accept; the rape of children happen every day to girls and boys. It happens. It is not an accident. It is not something that needs to be hidden away any longer. But sadly, we don't want to talk about it and in many ways, the result may be the decision of a child ending their life.

I'm that child, that grew into a boy in a man's body, that on November 2nd, 1994, found himself in Womack Army Hospital, Fort Bragg, NC., having nearly successfully completed his suicide attempt. Yes, I did it. Somehow, for reasons that I still don't understand, I didn't stay dead. I say "stayed" because my blood alcohol level was .314, plus, I had a stomach full of Percocet as a chaser. From what the doctors told me, I coded three separate occasions. Meaning, they had to bring me back three separate times. And for the record, you don't see it in the movies or television shows but, the paddles they use to revive you can leave actual burn marks on your skin. So yep, I was done with life.

I am that man that even after all of that, found a way to survive. So much so that I met an amazing woman that agreed to be my wife. She introduced me to conversations about Christ (more on that later) and in that, I was able to reevaluate and reconsider how I saw life. In the end, we got married and started a family. Though she was pregnant with someone else's child when we married, the birth of that child, *my* son, regardless of biology, was for me, a spectacular moment in my life. From his very first breath, I was in love with him. It didn't matter that his biological father wasn't me. It didn't matter. What mattered was how he breathed against me. How he rested against my chest those first few moments of his life. It was in that moment, within the marriage to a woman that loved me, with our child in my arms, that much of my life seemed to fall into place. Or so I thought.

Our second son Malachi was born May 20th, 1999. His death on July 31st, 1999, was the nail that shuttered and very nearly closed the whole of my heart and emotions. It sent me into a darkness that would very nearly destroy me. I will talk more about the death of my son later in this book but, for now, just know that his death set in motion a series of events in my life that I didn't even see at the time.

But events that would forever change who I am, what I believed and how I came to love life the way that I do now.

So there's my resume, my credentials if you will. I was that child whose parents thought violence was the proper way to instill discipline. I was that child that was sexually abused, that quiet one, that grew into a man without understanding about how to love and live in a way that lent itself to happiness and joy. I was that child so desperate for love and affection, that his own self-worth was so blurred that anyone who showed me a hint of kindness could have me for a cup of coffee and a gentle word. I was that child that was lost and lonely, that grew into a man emotionally incapable of relating to his wife or children, to such a degree that drinking was the go-to, the default ways and means of dealing with the world around him.

This book is for anyone, parent or child, young or old, that wants to live a life on their own terms. This book is for anyone that wants, or needs, to live, to love, to breathe in a way that grants true freedom and the hope that all of life, no matter how dark or shitty it may seem, is truly worth living. And living well.

During those times when you may think that I am meandering too far afield, have patience with me, for I promise you, there is a reason. And that reason, nearly every time, was not known to me while I was experiencing whatever it was that I was going through, but only in hindsight, was I blessed to be able to glean from those moments precious pearls of wisdom that played a critical part in my healing. Bear in mind, that sharing all of the tiny details is a way of my sharing the truth, as best as I can recall, and that in this sharing, it's my deepest desire and my hope that you might be able to relate.

So to you, my dear reader, know that in my heart, in my soul, I want you free. I want you to love and be loved. Not that conditional shit that people pass off as love that we so often see, that is supposed to act as the "real" thing. No. The kind of love that I am talking about, that kind that you deserve, whether you know it or not, or even if you don't believe it (yet), is the kind of love that liberates the soul from fear, and gives freedom to dreams and hopes that we've kept hidden away for fear that they might be trampled upon, tossed aside, ridiculed or crushed beneath the oppressiveness of hatred.

To you, reading these words, that may feel the sincerity and honesty in every word, in every sentence that I share with you, I want you to believe, to trust in me, to give me the benefit of the doubt, that I mean it when I say that I want you to look in the mirror and love the person that you see looking back at you, I mean it. I want you to know that every fiber of your being is a wondrous and beautiful creation. That you, yes *you*, are **fucking amazing** in ways that you can't even begin to fully imagine. Yet. But if you stay with me, and if you can trust me just a little bit, and if you can allow yourself just a glint of light, and a moment's reprieve from the negative voices in and around you, and *if you can stay with me through these pages,* you and I will discover together, that you deserve to be loved. Truly.

This walk that we will share is beyond what you've been told by others that didn't, wouldn't or couldn't see just how beautiful you are. This walk that you and I are going on, is one of love and unity, and it doesn't matter if you're transgender, gay, straight, short, tall, fast, slow, weak, strong, Black, White, male or female, or anything or anyone that has been mistreated, abused, bullied, attacked or hated. What matters to us, you and I, right here and now, in this very moment, is a walk together that's just about you and I.

I know what I'm saying is more than possible. I know for a fact, as living proof, that there is love to be shared, to be lived, to be given away, to be embraced, to rejoice within. And if you will trust me, just a little, I promise to share my life with you fearlessly and honestly, so that you and I might, together, show *you* that you too, are fucking amazing! Yes, I said, "*fucking amazing*" and I meant it.

I'm living proof.

So, let's Kick Rocks!

What do you really, *really* want?

Introduction

When I began writing this book, I struggled with how to begin this whole thing, who I was, am, how to introduce myself and what to include about myself. As I alluded to earlier, there was also the challenge of loyalty to family that I was, without really knowing it, still wrestling with; I had no desire to intentionally harm or injure others with the sharing of my story. I love my parents and had no desire to cast them in a negative light however, there was no way that I could honestly share my story without including the critical nature of my childhood and my upbringing. But since this whole journey is about healing and truth, I decided that my sense of loyalty would have to take a backseat. Along with that challenge, I realized the full import of my undertaking; people were going to read this book and in many ways, the trust in me was, and is, real. I wanted to make sure that the words on the page were words that meant something real, not only to me, but to every person that would trust me. It was that important to me.

Once I decided that I had to include key and critical aspects of my history that deep down, I really didn't want to share, I realized that there was the challenge of determining how much of my personal darkness needed to be shared. How much could, and should, or needed to be shared? Were there parts that really could be skipped, or glossed over? Since this isn't just a trip down memory lane, what then needed to be shared? Again, it was my deepest desire to harm no one, to not cast anyone in an undeserved negative light. But in the end, over the years of inward and personal struggles, I finally decided that those who love me, truly, would understand that my sharing is about sharing a healing process and not about vilifying or damaging the reputations of others.

As I said in the Preface, part of the process was acknowledging that on paper, that looking at my history laid out in categories and neatly arranged paragraphs, I was a hot mess. And it's the truth.

Nothing in my past, even the little that's available in the public record, gave one the confidence that I was a good person. But like so many things in life, the "facts" didn't tell it all, or come anywhere close to having revealed the whole picture. What the "facts" on paper didn't reveal was that I had lived through sexual abuse, emotional and physical abuse at the hands of my parents, homelessness, a suicide attempt (that was damn near successful), four DUI's, the death of an infant son, four divorces, and a host of other challenges of and in an emotional darkness that had nearly strangled the life from me. And yet, each of these experiences that couldn't be fleshed out on paper, when I finally understood, were the keys in sharing the journey with others that might be questioning, in their own life, how to find peace. And because I am now thriving, I knew that it was necessary to tell-it-like-it is/was. I will go into more detail within the body of this book later however, I wanted to mention these moments now so that you can get a glimpse of what is to come and more, how very serious I am about what it is that I am sharing.

I am thriving. I am loving. And I am loved. But it was not always so. I am well-aware that I am not the only person that has been through their own personal darkness. I am also fully aware of the fact that there are those that have lived through far more than I, and that have escaped far greater darkness and evil that I pray never to see. But none of this changes the life that I have lived, nor does it negate what I have learned over the years. In fact, were I able to talk with others that have overcome and transcended their own personal hells, I am sure that we would share much in common. I have lived through and in enough darkness to be able to say that I know what I'm talking about.

So, in the interest of full disclosure, let me lay this out in the simplest terms. This entire book is about my history and the steps and lessons that brought me to a place of peace. I share my history because I want you, the reader, to see and feel, to know and experience, as best as I am able to in the pages of a book, that which I went through, and in many ways, I share experiences that very nearly destroyed me because, for those that are reading this with hope, I want you to heal. To be free. To finally breathe. I rose beyond what could have destroyed me and despite the arguably damaging experiences of my past life, I am here to share, with you, my dear reader, the wonder that is, love.

This book is not a textbook, per se. This book is about the experiences, the choices and the forgiveness that had to take place for me to get to a place of not only peace but more, one of joy and happiness. The moments that I share in this book, taken deeply from my heart and soul, are shared as a hopeful inspiration that I dare to believe will encourage you to change the course of your life in positive, moving ways that, at times, almost seem otherworldly. This book is not about perfection, but of peace. These experiences, both mine and yours, are a path and journey to a life deserved, but perhaps not yet lived. This is not about being right, but about being free. Free to breathe. Free to love. Free to live. Being Real. Being Free. Being You. Truly, you.

The simplest way for me to explain the whole of this book and how I see and relate to life, and how I hope that it will resonate with you, is that we all have different paths, different experiences and different wants and needs. It's a shame, to me anyway, that we live in a world that wants to try and tell us that because we are a particular race, religion, or gender, or nationality, that somehow, we either should, or must, share the same view of life. I don't believe that. I just, don't. We can surely share some similarities but, in every way that matters, we are still not the same. I realize that this may seem self-evident however, I share this with you because I want you to know I don't want to assume anything, and I want you to know where I'm coming from and what my intentions are. But however you view this book, or the person behind the words – me – you are free to feel it, believe it and own it in any way that works for you.

Think of it this way; you have your own unique gifts and talents (whether or not you believe it, or have grasped onto that wondrous understanding is okay – it's there!) and this book is not designed to teach you how to paint, or meditate, or exercise self-hypnosis. I cannot teach you anything. I simply, cannot. More than that, that's not the purpose of this book. This book is an honest expression of one man's journey to finding and ultimately, learning the beauty of loving my true self. More than that, it is the story of so many of us. Though the details may differ, in the end, we are all nevertheless, joined in this journey called life. And through that, we share far more than most of us ever come to realize.

And if that's true, what's the point of you reading this book? If I am not going to give you the keys to the universe, so to speak, why should you read this little book? So, here it is, plain and simple: this is about inspiration. This book is not a textbook. This is not a step-by-step manual of any kind. There are no assignments, no homework and no empty, "inspirational" platitudes designed to fill up pages. And more importantly, there are no bullshit, made-up anecdotes designed to make a point, regardless of whether or not it's true. This is a conversation between you and I, and everything that I share here, is true. And because it's true, this means, that this is a shared experience between you and I. It's how I wrote it. It's how it lives in my heart and soul. I know that everyone is going to get something different out of this book, and because I know that, there is no point in me acting like I have the answers for everyone; I'm not that arrogant. In fact, some will think that they have wasted their money and will wonder why they even bothered in the first place. And that's okay. Because, like everything else in life, no two stories are the same. No two expectations are identical. No two people are the same.

But these stories I share with you, and what I learned from and through them, are shared in the hopes that you will be inspired to be, you.

This is an adult book that talks about adult experiences. The language, at times, will be of an adult nature; I have written this book honestly, transparently and with a personal expectation that the words in this book will reflect the words in my heart. If you meet me on the street, you just might hear me use the "f-bomb". It's not that I lack the intelligence, or the vocabulary to choose a different word rather, it's that sometimes a well-placed, honest use of the word "fuck" is on order. You may disagree, but again, like everything else in life, that's okay.

The language in this book is critical. I am being honest with you, not only in what I say, but in how I say it. I will not necessarily follow our prescribed methods of grammar and syntax, and I can assure you, at times, that the language will be colorful, to say the least. I do this because, for me, it has to be about honesty. And more than that, for many of us, in our own minds, in the conversations that we don't share with others, we speak to ourselves rather harshly. So the language I use is not random, any more than it's intended to merely shock; it's how so many of us talk to ourselves on the inside. It's how we relate to the world, inside, where no one can enter. It's in our deepest and darkest places, and it shades how we relate to the world. And ourselves. However polite we may appear to the outside world, for too many of us, the language that we use, with ourselves, is a reflection of how we feel and more often than not, when thinking of ourselves, or talking to ourselves, we are anything but polite.

So we get real in this book. Though I know that some of you may be offended by the use of the curse words/cussin'/swearin', I can assure you, it all comes from the heart. And if you think that the language choice somehow lessens the meaning of what I am sharing here, that's okay – perhaps this book isn't for you. It's not a requirement that everyone like me, let alone like everything that I am going to say. It's just how life is. And I'm more than okay with that.

But there is another, deeper reason that I have chosen to write the way that I do. For those of us that have struggled to find our happiness, we have encountered moments in life that weren't gentle. For some of us, propriety and decorum were a façade used by the tormentors, the bullies and those who had learned to melt into the world to cover their truest selves. For the well-dressed, articulate rapist that finds his pleasure in the violence of taking from another, that which was not, or is not, given freely. They have learned to walk about the world with handshakes and smiles, while in their hearts, they seek to destroy. Or the well-heeled, affluent bigot that hides his malice behind the trappings of polite society, while at the same time, he's abusing his wife and children with impunity. So no, not everything in this book is going to be "uplifting". Including the language. Because the truth is, not everything in life is gentle and pretty.

The point of this book, the real meaning behind it, is to share with others how you too can live as you truly desire, deserve and believe you want to live. We will do this together.

This book is for anyone that intuitively knows that something inside is not as it should be. It may be an awareness of their own inner chaos and darkness, and yet, they can't quite put their finger on what it is. Maybe they want off the merry-go-round of pain and suffering. This book is for any person, regardless of gender, social standing, wealth, success, race, creed or background, that feels trapped in pain, loss, grief, self-doubt, self-loathing, self-hatred or any other process or practice that keeps one in bondage. This book is for anyone that wants to love themselves and be free. Free from "what" is for you to decide. Perhaps it's smoking, or drinking, or those nameless, empty sexual encounters, or the need to hide behind a career… whatever it is, only *you* know the truth. And it's that truth that will either destroy your peace, or become a launching point into a life that you may have only dreamed of.

I speak frankly and openly. I am not here to try and impress you with my vocabulary or gift of "gab". Rather, it is my hope that the honesty I share here will be appreciated and understood rather than looked upon as being sensational or otherwise less than genuine. I am reasonably well-versed in acceptable punctuation, grammar and sentence structure, however, I chose to write this book the way I speak: sometimes chaotic, at times hard to follow, and not necessarily adhering to the rules. It will be disjointed, brash, crass, belligerent, but above all else, I will always be honest. It may seem to ramble at times, and really feel that a great editor might have made it easier to read. But this was a conscious and deliberate choice to share the whole and complete unedited journal entries, many of which are as chaotic and confusing to me now as I reread them, as they will be for you. But they needed to be shared.

I do not claim to be a prophet, a mystic, a priest, a know-it-all, or a grand leader of men. I don't claim to have discovered a new secret, nor some far and distant revelation previously hidden from mankind. Nope. What I am, is a man that has an ugly past that has not only come to terms with it but even more, is no longer a prisoner of it.

Together, let us begin this journey. Together, today, let us begin to unravel, deconstruct, review and disassemble that which opposes the true nature of who and what we are, and that which we truly desire.

Today, together, let us then take some time to reveal, discover, and breathe in that which we truly desire.

Love.

Chapter 1: Who is This Dude?

When I originally wrote the Preface and Introduction, they were not that long or that "revealing". This wasn't because I was necessarily afraid, or trying to hide anything but, in many ways, it was an exercise in giving myself permission to write in and with my own, true voice. I wrestled with myself, and eventually with others over how best to construct and order this whole thing. In the end, after about five years of wrestling with this thing and others, I finally decided to just do it, "my" way and just let the proverbial chips fall where they may.

I share this with you so that you can get a glimpse into the nature of how we all have to address our own acceptance and comfort in doing that which we truly desire to do, when we know that we're open to being "judged" by others. Were this not such a personal journey that I'm sharing, I wouldn't have had so many starts and stops, and would have been able to complete this all rather quickly.

But this is very personal. This is literally "me" in these pages. Here for you to get to know and in that....

I think that we tend to ask "who someone is", because we tend to think that we'll get some information to help us qualify if we like the person, or whether or not we might be able to trust what they have to say, or even them. But the truth is, there are any number of reasons that may, or may not, make any sense to anyone else in regards to answering that question of who we are. Truth is, the best that we can hope to do is present as honest a reflection of who we believe ourselves to be at any given moment in our lives. So we ask the question, and hope that we're able to give an honest answer. And that's provided we know who we really are.

I can say that I am a fifty-something year old Black man (born in St. Louis, in 1965), and since you can't "*see*" me, who's to know what you imagine I might look like; only *you* can know what you imagine, what you see in your mind's eye. Am I tall or short? Am I attractive or not? Do I have a beard, a mustache, or am I clean-shaven? My point is, most of these things are relative. Suppose you see me on a video, or come to a class that I am teaching. What might you think then? Though you would physically see me, hear what I have to say, be able to ask questions, interact with me and have a fuller impression of me than you would through just reading this book however, even that moment is not going to give you the fullness of who I am. Of who I have become. Or the lessons that I have endured, overcome, learned from, and that are an inseparable part of the fabric of my being. But there's something even more telling, and it's something that few people seem willing to admit.

We are ever-evolving. In many ways, I can say that I am not the same person that I was ten years ago. Ten years ago I would have had to include in my "resume" that I was a drunk. A reasonably functional drunk but, a drunk nonetheless. Interestingly enough, how did you picture a "drunk"? See my point?

So, who am I? It's my hope that what I share with you in these pages will do more than give you an idea of who I am, and have become. My sharing is really about specific moments in time that are critical to me, in my way of reflecting the life I am choosing to live, so that you can evaluate your life with a confidence and assurance that determining your worth and wealth of character, despite what others may have told you, or are telling you on a daily basis, and whether you believe it or not, is truly in your hands.

I wish that someone had spent time with me telling me, and perhaps even showing me, how beautiful and wonderful, unique and special I really am. I don't mean "better" than anyone else but more, that I was lovable. That I was a blessing. On a more frequent basis during my childhood, I ached to hear someone tell me just how wonderful I truly was and even, how much joy I added to their lives. How different would my life have been, if I'd had a parent, or any trust-worthy adult for that matter, that would have laid in the tall grasses with me, staring up at the clouds, and just spent time with me, sharing silence, or moments of imagination. How much closer would my father and I be, had we developed a relationship built on hugs, laughter, companionship and just, "being".

But let me clarify this, right now; this is not about whining, or bitching, or "wishing things were different". As best as anyone is able, including myself, this is about an objective reflection and discussion on *very specific* moments in my life for the specific purposes of sharing with those that are hurting. This is not a tell-all tear-down of any one person, including my father, nor is it meant to be a trip down "memory lane" for the sake of reminiscing, nostalgia or sentimentality. Though there are moments in my understanding that may have bits and pieces of each of these very human aspects of our nature, the intent of this book is not about destroying or demonizing another person. With that, understand that as a child, teen, and for most of my adult life, to me, my father was a brutal, heavy-handed, emotionally cold and distant, asshole – that's how I saw him. How I felt about him. But that was *my* perception, based on what he did and said, and how he treated *me*. But like everything else in our lives, it depends on one's own perspective and relative understanding of the world without, and the one within. For I am sure that my mother would disagree. And that's okay.

It was a sobering moment to realize, that no matter how I wrote part of this book, if I was going to be honest with you and me, that it was going to paint my parents as "bad" people. People that made mistakes but, were intelligent enough to have sought other ways and means of raising their children. But as I have been saying, and as is a foundation for the purpose of this book, when we reflect on the past, it should be to learn about ourselves, or from an experience in which we might find some precious pearl of ourselves that was missed. I know that this sounds utterly crazy, but I am asking you for your patience. Please.

I am going to share with you one of the most profound and life-altering experiences that I can recollect. As I share this, you may be tempted to hate my father. You may think of all the things that you would like to do, or say to him. And on the one hand, I get it. But this is not about punishing my father, or making him out to be a villain; this is really all about me. So I am asking you to withhold your judgment until I am finished sharing this particular moment in time. First though, there are psychological terms that I could define here but, I won't. For several reasons. But suffice it to say, that during my stints in counseling, I have heard such things as trauma, disassociation, torture, "Stockholm syndrome" and several others, but that is not what this sharing is about…. Just wanted to give you a heads-up.

I was in elementary school. Wedgwood Elementary in Florissant, Missouri, to be exact. I was in sixth grade, and I was not the kind of student that was all too comfortable with this type of public school. In short, because my parents had made the kind of sacrifices to send me to the best of schools. A private-school foundation at The Wilson School, a well-educated mother that read to me, taught me to read, and a father well-versed in what he believed a good education meant, gave me an educational foundation that I can honestly say, not many Black children were exposed to. So coming to this school, this suburban public school so unlike anything that I had experienced was a shock to me in ways that I couldn't even verbalize.

Why am I sharing this? What's the point? *What does this have to do with the stuff you were just talking about?*

Here I was, this well-educated, articulate, intelligent Black child that was thrust into a public school still wrestling with bussing in inner-city Black kids. I didn't fit in with the Blacks. I didn't fit in with the Whites. I felt so very, very alone. My grades suffered. I was lost. I didn't know how to articulate what I was feeling. We'd come from a land of plenty (in my mind), to living on the second floor of my grandmother's house. I know now, but didn't then, that my father had lost a high-paying job, had no insurance for the family and had had some dental challenges. I also understand now, on reflection, that there were stressors on my parents, particularly on my father, a proud, intelligent and dynamic Black man, that may have allowed him to enter a place that, had he been in another environment, caused him to take out his anger, frustrations and fears on his firstborn son.

Me.

I can't tell you about anything that my father and I talked about before, or after the incident that I'm now about to share. I can't tell you what day of the week it was, or really, the year (though, if I researched it, I could find out) but, what I do know, is that I was in sixth grade at Wedgwood Elementary. What I do remember is forever etched in my mind. And I share that moment with you now.

My father was wearing a white, ribbed A-shirt, or "wife-beater" as some call it. He was wearing polyester, in-style 1970's dark pants, dark brown, or perhaps black. He was not wearing socks. I don't know why I remember that detail but, he wasn't wearing his usual black, nylon business socks. And for the record, as I write this, I can remember how my grandparents house smelled. Sweat. Heat. Meals cooked over the last few days. Some fried chicken, onions and whatever other southern dishes had been made. 2016, I'm writing a book, thinking about that day, and I can still smell the house. The power of the imagination and moments in our past....

Whatever we talked about while we were in that room on the second floor, was drowned out by the sound of my heart beating in my ears. I remember that he made me strip down to nothing. No underwear. No tighty-whiteys were going to interfere with the spanking that was coming. But this time was different. Something about the whole thing was off. I had had spankings before but, there was something different about my father. Something was truly wrong.

A brown extension cord. He was talking, and for the life of me, I couldn't hear him. I could only watch as he wrapped that cord tightly around his right hand. I was trying to hide my little penis, my nakedness. I don't know why but, it just felt odd to be completely naked for a spanking.

The fucking sound that an extension cord makes when it slices through the silence. It's a "whoosh" sound, and it came out of nowhere. There was no warning. He just did it. I don't remember where it hit me but, the pain took my breath. It hurt so bad, and the pain came on so suddenly and deeply, that I wasn't even able to scream. I do remember running across the room and hearing him say, "don't you run from me" and then that sound again. The "whoosh". It was as if I was either running from the pain or trying to catch up with my own senses.

I tried to crawl underneath the bed. Another "whoosh". More breath stolen and the pain just kept coming. It was something hellish and wholly unknown. I couldn't get underneath the bed. There was no place to hide. To run to.

That fucking sound.

He told me that he was going to "beat the devil out of me". Then I felt/heard/experienced the feel of that cord hit my penis; I was awash with a soul-bending pain that, to this day, I have no words for.

I have lived through the death of a child, and as I write this, the thought of that extension cord and my father, that room and that beating, nearly cause me to cry. Even now. The power of memory.

But, in the midst of it all, suddenly, there was peace.

In ways that I cannot rationally explain (though I could go through the psychological theories that I referred to earlier, but won't), I remember that I was whisked across the room to find myself standing next to the window on the right. As I stood there, I was clothed. I was okay. But, as "normal" as I felt, I was watching this poor, poor child get the shit kicked out of him by his father. Even as a child, in that moment, I understood empathy and I did, truly, feel for that child and wished him such a better life to come.

I watched him roll into the fetal position as this bigger Black man continued to raise and lower the extension cord. I watched as that beating continued, and the child stopped crying and stilled; he just laid there and took it. Not moving. Not fighting. Not crying. Just, existing.

I am fifty-something as I write this, and I know how young I was when it all happened to me. I didn't know then, that I was the child watching my "self" get beat.

It changed me. It changed my life.

Whatever drove my father to do what he did, I cannot explain. I can offer what I think are reasons, based on what little I know of that time in our lives but, the truth is, you would have to ask him. What I do know however, is that the experience, however others may define it, caused me to become a different person than I otherwise might have become.

This is not about blame. I cannot speak as to why my father did what he did. I cannot tell you what he was thinking, or what his reasoning and justification might have been. In other words, I can't tell you why he did what he did, no matter how much I may speculate.

So whoever my father was on the inside, that's who he truly is and so much more than the man and actions that I share here in these pages. I cannot, in any way, quantify who he is as a person. But, I wanted to share that experience right now so that you will fully understand that outside of his actions with me, and the things that he told me in that moment, that I am in no position to call my father anything. Good or bad. The only thing that I can do is relate incidents that made a significant impression on me. No more and no less. If you want to know about my father, or anyone else for that matter, you would have to speak with them and come to your own conclusions. And finally, at least for now, I own every word, emotion, perception, impression, and idea that I write about on these pages and as such, it's not for anyone else to interpret for me either the truth or validity of what I share. And that includes my mother and father.

My point is, we must own our choices and hold ourselves accountable for the decisions we make, no matter how painful or joyful they may be. Yes, we may have people and circumstances that aid us in the decisions that we make but, in the end, we are the ones that make the decision.

What I can do, and is my right, is to take moments in my life and define them however I choose. And this choice is mine, and mine alone, unless I willingly choose to allow someone to be a part of the process. But even then, the choice is mine to do with my experiences and my memories as I see fit; no one has the right to take my truths from me.

And before you think that I've lost my mind in what I've just written, bear with me. I am not talking about a child choosing to be sexually abused; that's on the adult, not the child in any way, shape or form. I am not talking about a woman choosing to be raped; that's all on the rapist and his lack of understanding about the worth of life and love. No. What I am talking about are the inner conversations that we have with ourselves, those that we are aware of, and as a result, we must acknowledge our part and take ownership of the decision(s). What does the woman decide to do after she is raped? What decisions does she make? Does she decide to take back her power and prosecute? Or does she make another choice? These are not judgments, or head-shaking and finger-pointing; it's about having an honest conversation about objective and subjective truths and how they relate to *you*. Not someone else's view or truth, but *yours.* But more on that later. For now, nothing about what you and I are sharing right now, is about excuses or blame.

We want to be free, whole, loving and in love. Joyful and peaceful. Well and happy, and for me, this was a part of the process; taking back my personal power to truly live. And that meant dealing with life in a whole new way and it meant that I was going to have to decide on how I wanted to live the rest of my life.

A scary-ass proposition indeed.

I have seen and lived in the pit of my own personal hell.

I am now living a life that I thought to never know. I am, for myself and for anyone not yet willing to give up, living proof that love does indeed exist. And that it awaits us all.

The beauty of sharing my story with you, is that I don't have to convince you of anything. If you're breathing, if you're alive, if you're still with me through these words, then that means that you haven't yet given up hope that peace and happiness are possible. It doesn't, as you are well-aware, generally happen over night, that we become free of the emotional baggage that we've been carrying.

And though I never thought that I would be such a person, I am one that now knows the power of love, of being in love and the strength of forgiveness, that immeasurable depth of patience and longing to love all people. Through love, I began a journey of discovery such as I was never even able to believe or conceive. Through the blessing of Love, I now see and live a life that I never thought to ever see, or believe that I could ever deserve. Through the majesty and wonder of Love in this life that I treasure each moment of every day, and through this Love, in which I am awed daily, and by the ever-present knowledge that in this love, I am never a failure, but always a work in a progress.

And for the record, this isn't going to be a long, drawn-out love-fest, all wrapped in Kumbaya and good intentions. This is going to require some honesty on your part and a willingness to go deep inside to tell yourself a truth that you may not be aware of. I say that because, if you have those moments where you wonder "what's wrong with me," then you have a truth that you may not have yet acknowledged but nevertheless, is there.

Some may call this wonder of love and life, the power of God, or the universe, or by any other name there may be, I do not know; I just call it Love. But it's not the love that my parents or the world taught me. It's not the love that Hollywood would try and convince you it is. What I do know, is that there exists, in all of us, the power to live and love, that is beyond whatever limitations we have accepted as truth about who we are, in and through our past. This Love is not a religion, or a philosophy, or even some "meeting of the minds", but in all ways, it is neither created by, nor limited by religion, philosophy or processes; we, you and I, are the power-center through which this Love is made manifest.

So you and I are going to head along together in this journey. I truly hope from my heart, that something you will read within the body of this book will touch you, that will perhaps allow you a moments reflection that leads to *your* peace and freedom. This is not to say that everyone who may read this will find something of import, or that everything here will provide you with answers to any question that you might have. I do not share my story with the intent of offering you specific answers for *your* future, rather, it is my heartfelt hope that you will see in me, something within *you*, that can help *you* define your roadmap to *your* idea of peace.

The world and all that it encompasses has changed for me. It has not been an "easy" road, nor is the journey over. What I say, without hesitation or remorse, is that I now look forward to what my tomorrows hold for me. I can smile now, knowing that the smile is my own, that it is now a frequent and welcome member of all that I have come to be. That doesn't mean that everything, in every moment, is perfect but, it means that I now know that it's not as bad as it may seem either. I have a process, a plan and purpose to which I am committed and in that, I have found life.

And Love.

Finally, let me add this for those of you that would like to break this book down, analyze it, critique and then evaluate to some point where you believe that you have enough information to quantify and qualify whether or not what I share is true. Well, here ya' go –

This is my life. This is a life that I have lived and over the course of many, many years, I have learned so very, very much about what it means to love myself. I have, with every fiber of my being, come to conclusions that do not require your approval. I have learned, through experience and life, that who I am, is not contingent upon whether or not everyone believes, agrees, confers and decides on the merits of my story. I have written this book because I know that there are others who, as I once was, suffer greatly for not seeing themselves worthy of being loved. So, for those of you that would seek to tear down and destroy what I share here, I say, have at it. Do your best. And from my heart, with all the love and respect I bear, you may respectfully, Kick Rocks.

Ultimately, I can offer you no more than this; myself.

We all, regardless of our pasts, what has been done to us, what we may have done to others, deserve to love and be loved.

This includes you.

One of the things that you'll pick up on very quickly as you read this little book, is that I repeat things often. This is not to fill up pages but rather, it serves a very real purpose for me. I know that some of you will get a little tired of reading the same things but, part of why I do that is to illustrate a point that I will talk about later. But for now, bear with me, and we'll get through it.

But let's tell it like it is, even more. I didn't always see the world as a kind place. I didn't always believe in the idea of love, let alone that it was for me.

On November 1, 1994, I awoke like any other morning. There was nothing particularly different that day. I was in the US Army, stationed at Fort Bragg, NC and had recently had knee surgery for damage that had gotten progressively worse over the previous few months. But the day itself, that morning, on the outside, was like any other day. I can still remember that it was a bright morning. It was not yet hot, but the sun was bright. So bright, in fact, that I actually decided to wear sunglasses. Wearing sunglasses was a rarity for me. Since I needed prescription sunglasses and had none, as those were a luxury and expense that I couldn't afford, the idea of wearing non-prescription was really quite foreign to me.

But on that morning, I really didn't care that the glasses I wore weren't prescription, I just knew that I wanted to wear sunglasses. Though the world was remarkably fuzzy, and I knew that in very short order, I was going to have a headache, I didn't care. Not that morning. I had opened the small fridge that was provided for us, and had taken out a Colt 45 forty-ounce beer that I purchased the night before, and I began to drink. Early in the AM, I was getting my drink on; it was a special day. As I look back on that day, I don't know if I needed the sunglasses to allow myself to drink that early in the morning, or if I had reasoned that it was the weekend, I didn't have duty and that meant that I was free to do whatever I wanted to. So with that ridiculous bit of "logic", it had been decided that it would be a "sunglasses inside", cold beer and no-care's-on-my-mind kind of day. After having had the knee surgery only weeks before, I'd been limited to what I could do physically anyway, so what difference did it make that I was going to be drinking so early in the morning? I drank, and drank…. And drank some more. I drank like it was a professional responsibility, well into the afternoon.

And when I'd felt that I was drunk enough, I was ready for phase two.

Knee surgery provides one with plenty of pain pills. Percocet were the pills that I had been given. And they were going to be used to really "kill" the pain.

In the early morning of November 2, 1994 I was admitted to Womack Army Hospital with a blood alcohol level of .314 (that is point-three, not point-zero-three, well above the legal limit) and a stomach filled with Percocet, a rather effective painkiller. For all intents and purposes, I was DOA, as in, (literally) dead-on-arrival. I don't remember anything about that morning at the hospital. At all. I would later learn that CPR had to be performed, that I was not breathing, nor did I have a heartbeat when I was rushed into the ER. I was also told that I had been shocked with paddles (which explained the ugly burn marks on my chest). I was dead, plain and simple. I spent the following three days in and out of this life on earth, of which I remember nothing; I had to be told by the hospital psychiatrist what had happened.

Because I don't have any memories of a white light, or anything else, there is a very real part of me that wishes I could tell you that I was greeted by my long departed relatives, all there to guide me through to the other side. But if it happened, I honestly don't remember it. There was no light at the end of the tunnel, no claws of demons reaching out for me. I was just, gone. Not there. But even as I think back on that incident, I would like to say that once I was released from the hospital, that I had become a changed man. But two weeks after my release from the psych ward (which is where I was deposited after recovering in intensive care), I was once again back to drinking as hard, if not harder, than I had in my life before. Not to mention the fact that I was now really angry with a God that hadn't just let me die, that hadn't allowed me to be done with this earth. That's what I thought I had wanted; to die. To end the pain of living.

But how had I found myself in such a state? What had happened in my life, and to me, that had allowed me to reach such a dark place of pain and despair? I didn't know at the time, as I do now, but, at that time in my life, I wasn't really able to ask the questions that needed to be asked and addressed, let alone hear the answers.

Alcohol. I knew it well. In fact, one of the reasons that I didn't pursue writing this book years ago, is that I had actually wondered if I could even write well without having had a drink or two in me. Until I made some life-altering decisions about who I was, I never wrote anything without drinking. Drinking seemed to free the creative juices, made the process easier and provided me with a conduit to the emotions and creativity that I otherwise didn't believe I could have found within myself without the aid of the drink. I believed myself a more focused, more in-tune writer when I was well into a six-pack. Or twelve pack. Or whatever else happened to be around.

I was a solitary drinker. My preference had been to drink alone, with my favorite music on, the lights down low and the world beyond my window comfortably silenced by headphones. When the sun finally set and the sounds of the world around me had faded to virtually nothing, that was the time when I knew I could be free to drink as I wanted. To find that safe, secure place that I could only seem to find while I was either drinking or after I was good and drunk, had been a seemingly never-ending pursuit, and one that I had convinced myself was a part of what made me who I was, and something that I was never going to be able to shed. But what I hadn't understood at the time, was what I thought was to have been a lifelong pursuit, and not necessarily one that I had chosen for myself, but something that seemed to have found me, was in fact, just my way of keeping myself hidden and safe from my own "self"; one that I hadn't yet been able to acknowledge, let alone, accept.

Once I found that safe place in the drink, I would do whatever it took to maintain that state of "peace". In those moments, that's all that I ever thought I wanted. All I thought I truly needed was a safe place where I didn't have to feel any pain. A place where this God that I had been taught to fear and obey would really love me. That this hateful, vengeful being would not despise me, as I despised myself. In those moments, in my drunkenness, that was the place where I was safe, and the world outside could no longer hurt me; my drunkenness was a state and place of safety. A haven. A place where I was forever safe. When drunk, I could always find a place where dreams were supported by those people that claimed to love me. In those drunken spaces, dreams were possible to touch and not just "things" to be torn apart, analyzed and shown just how impossible or impractical they were. In my drunkenness no one spoke of my hopes and dreams, or that to have ever believed in the possibilities of their truth, as being utter nonsense. In those moments just on the edges of passing-out, I wanted to believe things like, "dreams really do come true." How I had wanted to shout to them all, "why can't you just love me and help do it instead of always shooting me down?"

When I drank, I could feel what I thought was love. When I drank, I believed that I could actually embrace my idea of love, let it wrap itself around me and tell me that I wasn't a bad person or the fuckup I believed myself to be. That I wasn't the piece of shit I believed and thought myself to be. That I was worth the effort of loving, worth the trial and the trouble of getting to know, of caring for, and more, that I was okay just as I was; that I didn't need to change in any way. How I longed to hear those words, to feel them real in my heart and soul. To have breathed life into those very real emotions, the ones that I was hiding from, and to have them made my own, was something that I had told myself I really wanted. And yet, no matter what I had tried, I was never able to find the courage to pursue or actually live what it was that I thought I needed and wanted. Whether within, or without my imagination, the truth of it was, at that time in my life, the effort and risk needed to be the real "me" was something that I didn't think I possessed. Or would ever have. I was searching for something that I could never lose, but at the same time, could never possess. I was seeking to find and live a love that I could hold onto and never have to return. But was too afraid to really believe that it existed, and if it did, was more than I deserved.

Pieces of shit like me, didn't deserve happiness.

Or love.

When I drank, I tried to convince myself that I was free to love my sons in a way that I thought was okay and right. That somehow, no matter who the true me was, I could love them in a way that didn't harm them, or destroy the beautiful people that they were. While drinking, or drunk, I didn't have to wonder if I was manly enough, or if I was the provider that my wife believed that I should be, or was supposed to be. When I drank, I was in an emotional place where the alcohol shaded me from the light of reality, and I was able to smile freely and tell my sons that their father, though flawed and imperfect, loved them the best that he knew how. When I drank, it was so very easy, I believed, to say to them, quietly, gently and sweetly, that I wasn't sure if I knew what love really was, but that in all ways that I knew, I loved them. That there was nothing that I wouldn't do for them in this world. That I would show them the wonders of the world, allow them to explore the world around them with the certainty that upon their return from the explorations, their father would be there waiting for them with open arms. Always. But even then I didn't realize the fallacy under which I had been operating.

Drunk is not a pathway to happiness. It is an empty, bullshit illusion to which hopes become temporarily affixed and wrapped within the false belief that we are more than we believe ourselves to truly be. For when we arise from our stupor, we are confronted once again, with the understanding and knowledge, that we yet remain, as we believed ourselves to be. *Unlovable.* One does not get drunk because one loves oneself.

Once the alcohol had its way, I no longer felt anger at the God I had been taught about. When I was in that hammock of high, I could temporarily convince myself that my parents, my wife or anyone else I believed didn't really love me, while drunk, they were my best friend and staunchest supporter. In that place where alcohol and I communed and supped, there was safety. There I was drunk as hell, and feeling that I was free of everything that otherwise weighed me down. I was free from having to remember the fact that I didn't like myself. Yes, and while drunk, I was able to even consider the idea that *loving myself was not a foreign and frightening concept.* Because for me, while sober, in my mind and heart, I truly believed that I had no knowledge or experience of love. But even while I was drunk and incoherent, to the point of blackouts, there were still those moments and times when I had to wrestle with the knowledge that I didn't feel deserving of love; the drinking didn't wash away the sadness and loneliness and realization that I was a piece of shit.

I tried to convince myself of all the times when I felt what I thought was love and wanted to recapture and hold onto those moments. The problem for me was that I just couldn't remember it when I wanted to remember. Instead, I could vividly remember, in great and graphic detail, how I came to dislike myself. How I came to hate myself enough to attempt suicide. These things, the hatred, anger, fear, loneliness and the failures, yes, those were things that I knew well. For in it all, somewhere deep in my heart, I believed that I knew how I came to be so afraid of life.

Much of what I believe about love was clearly defined for me during incidents that took place when I was a child. Though I have looked back at those times and have come to terms with them, there were still moments from those years, where I could not get beyond their meaning and the defining impact, on not only my self-image, but on my whole view of the world all around me. But even as profound as I thought those moments were, and through what I thought I had learned from them while I was experiencing them, I did not yet know that those moments were only some more of the beginning steps on my path to healing and happiness. There was so much more to learn and experience. To know. To accept. To embrace.

So much more life to live....

Pain is something I know well. Pain is something I can handle. Pain is just a thing, like drinking a glass of water. A thing that I can beat. So therefore, love, if it doesn't cause pain, isn't real. In the world that I knew, how could it be love if it didn't cause me to go well outside of myself to those places of safety that I had come to know and create over the years? How could it be called love if there was no associated pain? The kind of pain that shakes one's spiritual foundation and clings to you even after the act itself had ended long, long ago? I was wrong in what I believed, but I wouldn't know that for years to come.

My father called it discipline and spankings. What I can say now, at this stage of my life, in light of my experiences, is that which they, my parents, called a spanking was far more than that. Was my father a violent man? Not necessarily. But he had some ideas about child-rearing and discipline that were wrong. No matter how well-intentioned he may have believed himself to be, and against the life that I live now, one could argue that his methods lent themselves to my growth. However, what I can say is that it took many, many years to unravel his ideas and methods and come to a place of peace and personal acceptance of self. I will touch on these matters later in the book however, suffice it to say, that much of the critical ways I saw myself and the world around me were formed by the teachings of my parents.

I was in seventh grade, around thirteen years old, and he was the "guy" next door. I was soon to be thirteen and looking forward to being a teenager, while he was nineteen. I was small. He was large. I was a shy, introspective child that just wanted to fit in and not even sure what I wanted in life. He was a man. He already knew what he wanted, where he fit in, and he wasn't shy about it. For all the world to see, including my parents, he was just a nice guy that lived next door. One that no one would have thought of as a predator. He befriended me and no one said a word to me about it. At all.

I was a loner and was not one to open up to people easily, and he took up those spaces in my heart that so desperately wanted to belong to someone, to be wanted and needed, and more, cared for. Months passed, our friendship deepened and I began to see him as someone that I could trust. He'd never ever, laughed at me, never tried to take anything from me, or make me feel small on the inside. I could talk to him about anything and everything. So it seemed only natural when he asked me why I didn't like my father, and for me to tell him the truth as I knew it then. He'd listened so intently, telling me that everything was going to be okay. A hug, that not only seemed natural, but at that moment in time, it seemed to be something that I really needed and that's what he offered. A hug. Just a simple, caring hug.

When he put his lips to mine, it was odd but not unpleasant.

Though I didn't want it, I didn't want to lose my friend and after all, it wasn't hurting me to kiss him (it was my very first kiss). When he pressed his tongue against my lips, and I pulled away, he looked at me as though I had just killed a basket of pet kittens. And to this day, I have not forgotten his words, "it's okay, this is how it's supposed to be. I like you. I like you a lot." By God, that was what I needed to hear. That's what I wanted to feel. I wanted to be loved. I wanted to have that sense of belonging, that new feeling course through me for all time. So when he asked a thirteen-year old boy to take his clothes off, so that he could show me what "true love" really was, that thirteen-year old boy had hesitated, had wanted to run far, far away, but that boy had wanted to be loved even more than he wanted to run way. So that boy, me, did as he asked.

There is a pain to anal rape that is breathtaking. This wasn't a consensual date, where both of us had agreed to sexual expression. This was not even an agreement between two people capable of making a rational decision about sex. That was a man, that took advantage of a child. When a man forces an object up and into your anus, your asshole, whether a brush handle or a stiff cock, there is a soul-penetrating pain that literally takes your breath away. The moment he put the head of his cock against my anus, I wanted to run, to disappear, to just dissolve away. But with every centimeter that he pressed into me, the best I could do was cry into the pillow; he weighed so much more than I did.

I cannot honestly tell you how long it lasted that first time. And in truth, how long each of the subsequent rapes lasted. It's just what happened and in many ways, it became my normal. But something that I hadn't thought of until a friend asked me about what it was like when the rapes were over, was that, when he came, when he'd ejaculated inside me, was that he'd laid on top of me and told me that he loved me. Yes. He did. He said, with a beating heart and chest, caressing my right thigh, as though we'd just made love, that he loved me. He'd said it, and then kissed my right ear and then, my cheek.

How numb physically and emotionally must I have been to have forgotten those details? How he'd kissed me and told me that he loved me. How some part of me wanted to believe that he did love me. Surely, there must be something about love in all of this, right?

He'd pulled out, slapped me on the ass, and sat on the edge of the bed. And yes, I do remember, that he used my little underwear to wipe his cock off….

No one was there to help me stop crying. No one was there to help me understand why I felt that something inside me had fled. No one was there to explain to me why I thought that I was dying. I couldn't think. I could only see the tallest grasses in the fields in Columbia, and I could hear the sound of, nothing. There was nothing to hear. He just, sat up and left me there. Ah, but I was smart enough to keep the sounds of my crying to myself. My father had taught me that. I was taught well how to keep my tears to myself.

But rape is not just about physical pain. A rape, in every conceivable way, is a loss of power and identity. It is an emotional attack. It is a psychological assault. You are reduced to an object, and an object of little to no value. For those of you that have never been raped, there are no documentaries, no made-for-tv-movies that even begin to portray the fullness of rape. How can you demonstrate and share the depths of isolation so deep and profound that it literally takes away your ability to breathe, to think, to feel?

For those that have experienced this violation, when we're asked, "how do you feel?" or "how did it make you feel?" on so many levels, are questions to which we, more often than not, simply have no effective way to answer. It's not a matter of not wanting to, or not realizing or feeling the emotions (or lack thereof), it really comes down to no effective language skills to share the whole of that loss. Why loss? A loss of self. A loss of trust. A loss of belief in hope, the future. Loss of innocence. Loss of trust. And the list goes on. Does everyone experience it the same way, with the same results? Absolutely not. But I believe, with all that I am, that we all share something very real and very true; we will never be the same again.

No amount of therapy, no level of education and no amount of money, prestige or success is ever going to give back that which was stolen. This isn't to say that life won't ever be a joyous journey (as this book and I are proof that there is life to be lived and loved) but, we will always know that something was taken that we can't get back. Anymore than a dead child is ever going to return, the person we were, before the rape, is gone. Never to return. That must be acknowledged and accepted. We must allow ourselves, in this process, to mourn, to grieve, to be angry – to be pissed – or sad, or whatever it is that we truly feel. We must allow ourselves to live in a way that allows for us to emotionally recognize and acknowledge the truth of those moments and how they affected us then – and later in life – and in our every "now" moment. But these changes that we attribute to the ugliness done to us, that we experienced, that we lived through, as dramatic as they may have been, or even as real as they still feel at times, they are, in no way, *who we are*. A truth that no one told us, is that *we are not the sum total of the violence done to us*. In this, we begin the process of healing.

We are not perpetual victims. We are not the "survivor" of rape, or the death of our loved ones. We are so much more than the torment that would otherwise haunt us and keep us from the fullness of life and love.

I was trying to think of effective analogies, or comparisons to share with you that might better help you understand the destruction that is rape, and the truth is, I could find nothing. Trying to describe the effects of rape is like trying to describe the feeling of losing a child; we lack the words and mental and emotional functions to fully ever express those feelings to others when it comes to the death of a child. And sadly, in many cases, those that need those mystical words said the most, are those that are dealing with that death. But we simply don't have the words. And so it is rape. There is not a vernacular or language created that can express what it is to be raped.

And now, let me address something that I believe is critical. When you are the victim of rape, it is never, ever your fault. I don't care what anyone has told you, it was not then, and is not now, your fault. What many people that "victim-blame" don't, or won't understand, is that the victim of rape did, in that moment, what they believed they needed to do to make it to the next breath. And the one after that, in hopes that the rape would end. But in the meantime, it's a matter of doing whatever you believe you must do to just, live. It's not about "fighting back", or not doing everything possible to prevent it. It's not about somehow "wanting it", or having done something to arouse the attacker. It's not about the wrong or right clothing, or being too friendly, or saying the wrong thing, or being in the wrong place at the wrong time. It's never, ever about the victim.

I don't care if you've posted naked pictures of yourself on *every* social media platform ever invented. *Nothing* in your behavior, your thinking, or life means that you did anything to deserve being raped. I don't care what the world may say, what your families may have tried to do to keep the world from knowing, you were not to blame. For any of it. I don't care if you're "too young" to know anything about sex, or if you're a successful, independent professional on the outside for all the world to see, you did nothing to deserve being raped. Rape is not limited to a single gender; hatred should never be defined or limited by the outlet or victim – hatred is its own definition and the victim should never feel that they are somehow a variable of or for consideration as to having anything to do with it happening.

If you have ever been raped, I want you to right now, in this very moment (if you haven't already done so), allow for the possibility that you can forgive yourself for ever having been harsh with yourself. Or for trying to convince yourself, no matter how faint the accusations, that you were somehow a party to the violence that is rape, and that you had anything to do with it happening to you. Begin, in this moment to allow yourself to mourn, to weep, to acknowledge that someone took from you a very precious part of who you are, without your permission, without your consent. But, no matter how vile, degrading or painful it was, *they didn't destroy you.* By virtue of the fact that you're reading this book, that means that you *never* gave up. The fact that you're still here means that you still have hope. No matter how small it may be, it is still there.

And now, if you didn't already know it, you're not alone. Ever again.

For me, after the rape, the sodomy and the abuse, in my head, I thought I understood even less about what love was supposed to be. Such consistent betrayals of trust had taught me that my worth was defined by other people and more, that their definition was always based in part, on the idea that taking something from me was crucial to their being able to live their life the way that they wanted. I don't mean to imply that this understanding was correct, however, it was my perception, which in turn, meant that it was my reality and how I saw and related to the world. For some reason, I wasn't able to escape the utter and complete confusion that I felt about it all; I couldn't find that doorway to peace and comfort that exceeded the emotional isolation that I was feeling. The worst part for me at that time, is that I didn't have names for what I was feeling and experiencing. I had no knowledge of the deeper meanings of the rape that I had endured. So I was left to feel it. To take it. To live within the pain and confusion, hopelessly lost, and seemingly bereft of anything resembling normalcy.

I do not share this with you for the sake of gratuitous illustration, but rather, I want you to understand the complexities of all that I encountered and how I pieced together the meanings in my own mind. The physical pain itself, when one is raped anally, is literally enough to take one's breath away. So much so that you can't even scream in the beginning. So much so that you have no reference points with which to compare the pain; it is a pain unto itself that should never be experienced. The way I was treated in those moments, and the things that he said, the very words and the language, coupled with the act itself, and the overwhelming pain it caused both emotionally and physically, in that moment, diminished me as a person instantly. As it was happening, no one had to tell me, in words, though they were certainly said, that I was worthless; it was an immediate answer and validation as to who I believed myself to be as a person, that I was not a person. I was an object.

It taught me further, that I wasn't worthy of being loved, cared for or treated with any semblance of decency and kindness. In those moments, I believed, with every fiber of my being, that I was every disappointment to my parents. I was, while beneath him, with his cock in my virgin ass, every less-than-perfect grade that I had ever made. While he sought his sexual release, and my emotional denial, I was the nigger in the corner that takes the verbal barbs as being my due. I had become, in the moment of that invasion, all the worst that I could have ever imagined I could be. And the worst of it was, that I truly believed that I deserved it. In those moments, for me, pain had once again, equaled love.

I could continue with the events and actions that took place after that incident, but the details mean less to me than the resulting image I had of myself. I could talk about seeking love in bars, the many, many one-night stands. I could talk about the numerous empty relationships, all based on false premises not only about love, but of myself as a person. For who in their right mind was ever going to be able to love someone like me if they knew the truth? And who in their right mind would want to have a relationship with someone such as I? Who in the world was going to want damaged goods? What woman was going to respect and love a man with my history? Was I gay? No. But I'd had sex with a man, so I must be gay, right? It didn't matter then, nor does it now, that I was a child being taken advantage of by a predator. What matters is that what was done to me, caused me to question everything, as an adult, I ever thought I knew about safety, trust, love, sex, sexuality, belonging, right and wrong. How was I to even know to ask, or question such things as a thirteen-year old boy?

Then I had to contend with the maelstrom of mental confusion and emotional chaos all through my teen years and into some semblance of adulthood. And through all of it, in my mind, the only way that I could prove my sense of being as a "man", was to allow myself to have sex with as many women as possible as proof that I was not that which I could not escape; the fear that my sexuality had been turned upside down and into something that was sin, that was the antithesis to everything I had been taught that a man was, or was supposed to be. The very act of rape was one of loss on so many levels. In my mind, what person would offer friendship to one such as I, if they knew the whole truth? I was damaged and unworthy of love. That is what I believed. So much confusion. So much hurt. Pain.

Knowing, or at the very least, believing that no one would or could love me if they knew the truth, I learned to create a history for myself. It wasn't necessarily a conscious choice to create a false history, so much as a self-preservation and emotional defense mechanism. Rather than take the risk of being discarded because of truth, I simply remember being asked about my past and the next thing I knew, I was reciting a history and past to which I didn't belong and didn't belong to me. And yet, as unreal as it may have been in the telling of the lies, it was nevertheless a full history. It was a detailed yarn, an intricate, rich Rockwell-esque image of peace and happiness. A history wholly and completely separate from the one that I knew to truly be. A history that conveniently left out all of the "pertinent" factual details of my past. It was a history that served to not only release me from the pain of memory, it allowed for the active participation of the listener in that they could sympathize comfortably with the minor details that I did leave in, without having to know the deepest, ugliest aspects of the truths I held deeply and privately to myself.

I learned to be a consummate liar. The great fabricator. The reality of my life, the truth, the real truth, the one that I kept to myself, that I had accepted as mine and mine alone, and therefore, something that I was not going to speak of, and would remain hidden. So I became the best of liars. I could weave a story of such great detail that even I could believe my own bullshit. So well detailed were my stories, that I felt like perhaps, I really was that person that had lived the idyllic life that I spoke of. I tried to convince myself that I cared little for the fact that ultimately, when the truth was revealed, I would be shown to be a liar. No, for me in those moments, it was far better to lie and paint a false picture than to reveal the truth. I just wanted to be loved. At any cost. But for me, there was too much danger in allowing anyone to know the broken and busted person that I believed myself to be.

Over the years, I learned that I needed to weave enough truth into my bullshit so that I could avoid the painful discovery that always inevitably came as a result of absolute lies. But nevertheless, I still believed that I needed to share just enough, but not too much, of the real truth. It was a proverbial balancing act every moment, of every day. It had to be enough of the truth for me to share, to help them see the path that I had been on but, not so much that they could see just how truly screwed up I was. And more than that, I had learned that too much of the truth could be used as a weapon against me, to further make me feel like shit. Somewhere deep inside me, I needed to hear the listener's outrage, their utter disbelief that someone would do such horrible things to a person as nice as I. Good Lord, the tapestry of fear and loathing that I created within myself in those years....

What I wanted from them, what I thought I needed from them, was to be accepted in their eyes and I was more than willing to lie, steal and cheat to have that acceptance. It never occurred to me that there could be no real acceptance when the whole of it was based on lies. But I was willing to lie to be loved, or at least have the facsimile of it, as I had dreamed it could be. But the worst part about it was that I didn't know how to tell the truth without the anxiety and fear of being shown worthless and undeserving of love and kindness. How could I be loved for a person that I wasn't, for a person that I had created, perhaps based on a form of the truth, but not the truth as it truly was? I know now, and I think that subconsciously, I knew even then, that I couldn't have been wholly and fully loved based on a lie. But in the short-term, it seemed to give me hope and some semblance of happiness.

But inside of my soul, where I knew the truth lay, and the pain of lying resided, and in knowing the truth about myself, it was only natural *for me* to find something to fill the holes, and to silence my conscience. Alcohol served as a means of burying the truth even deeper, at least in the moment while I was drinking. Alcohol was a way of granting me a temporary, if not imaginary haven from having to look at myself too closely and for too long. The power of the drink had amazing medicinal uses for me. And in that "power", I would watch my life disintegrate before my eyes in the coming years. It would fall apart in such ways, that it would literally take years for me to heal. Though I didn't know what was coming in the years to come, and I couldn't have prepared for it even if I had known what it was, alcohol would come to play an even bigger part in my emotional and psychological demise.

Realizing that everyone's experiences are different, and as a result, responses are different, I know that not everyone will agree with my assessment of the shit that we've experienced. But remember the foundational tenets of this book; I am sharing my experiences, with my understanding, with my beliefs and my personal results so that you, if you are ready, can do the same thing. This is about inspiring you to be free enough to live life on terms that you define for yourself. In other words, it's my hope that my sharing, my observations may lend themselves positively to you defining the life you want to live. Redundant? Repetitive? Same thing said in different ways? Yep, absolutely – that's how important this is.

What was going to happen to me would be so profoundly painful, that it would even eclipse the childhood physical abuse and the rape. It would be so deeply traumatic and emotionally paralyzing, that it would fundamentally reshape and mold the whole of my awareness of and about life. It would cast a shadow over any notions or ideas that I had about love in ways that I could never have imagined. It would cause me to have such a breakdown that I would inwardly pray for death. It was a moment in time that I would hope that no person ever experience. Ever.

Chapter 2: How Low Can You Go?

NOTE - You will notice that I use the word/term God. This is based on my perspective and as a result, you will note that sometimes I capitalize God, and sometimes I don't capitalize, god. This is not to be cute but rather, it serves to literally underscore the confusion that I felt while I was experiencing so much pain and hopelessness. I know that it is not "normal" and that it can create some confusion while you're reading. But as much as I wanted to correct it, I fought my desire to do so, and in that, I hope that you can get an idea of just how utterly lost I was during this time in my life. I had to do it this way because quite honestly, I didn't then, nor do I now, have the words to even begin to express and explain that time in my life. – Chase

When I found my infant son, his body was cold and stiff. His little brown eyes were half open, and his lips were slightly parted, as if he were about to sigh, or whisper a secret to me. Tiny hands balled into fists, his left fist raised above his head, as if he were celebrating victory. I looked at him, and nothing registered. I thought that I knew he was dead, but that wasn't possible because I still had to make breakfast for him and his brother. Was I being irrational? Why was I thinking about breakfast? Oh, well, he had to be hungry, right?

The god that I believed in did not visit death upon infants. He did not extinguish life without explanation. He did not do things like that. No. No. No. I had to feed his brother. I had to make breakfast.

In my heart, the guilt was immediate and breath-taking. In my mind, I could only see that I had been the one responsible for his care and I had somehow failed to protect him. I had failed so miserably, so completely, that he had died. Though he died of SIDS, I knew, in my heart, why he had *really* died. For me, in my heart, in the darkness of my own soul, as it was at that time in my life, I believed, truly, that I knew that had I been a better person, my son wouldn't have died. For me, in every way that made me the man that I was at that time, I believed, with every ounce of my being, that my son died because I hadn't loved him enough.

Had I loved him strong and right enough, he would have lived. Had I been a better person, God wouldn't have taken him from me. Had I been…better.

Had I loved him enough and in the right way, the way a father is supposed to love a son, I would have checked on him before I went to sleep. Had I loved him enough, I would have held him and told him how much I loved him, rather than thanking God that he was asleep and not crying or demanding my attention and my marginal skills as a father. Had I loved him enough, I wouldn't have been selfishly thinking that all I wanted was the peace and quiet that his little lungs seemed to disturb at the most inopportune times. Had I loved him enough, had I not been so damned selfish, he would still be here.

Had I been a better person, one not so selfish, one that was open-hearted and free with affection and tenderness, gentleness and grace, I could have shown him the best in life. Had I not been so emotionally withdrawn, I would have been the kind of father that relished the moments of holding my son in my arms. I could have, should have been, the kind of father that danced with him in the living room, or played with him out in the yard. Instead, I was so far removed emotionally from my family, that I preferred drinking over spending time with such a demanding little person. My resentment of the love that his mother showered him with, was so palpable and tangible, that I had actually been jealous. What kind of father was jealous and resentful of an infant, and the relationship he had with his mother? What kind of horrible, messed-up, asshole felt such things?

When I found him, I could only look. I could only stare. When I found him, I couldn't speak. I couldn't believe. I couldn't.

When I found him, his lifeless body cool and stiff, his little brown eyes half open, his tiny fists balled, I wanted nothing more in my life than a moment to have gone back and traded my life for his. That was the right thing; trade my shit life for his life of innocence.

But there I stood and did the only thing that I could do, in my mind at least; I just held him, waiting for him to wake up. Wake. Up.

Realization of the truth hit me so hard, that I fell to my knees and released a sound from my soul that I hope to never hear again in this life.

There are no words that can describe the overwhelming pain, the deep, stomach-churning, breath-stealing pain that washes over you once your brain and heart register that your child is dead. Dead.

I wanted nothing more in my life, in that moment, than to have been given a chance to go back and trade my life for his. That was the right thing; trade my shit life for his life of hope, of promise. Of innocence. Innocence that I didn't have.

I had been through Combat Medic school in Fort Sam Houston, Texas, and I knew what had to be done but, please believe me when I say that, I knew intellectually that he was dead and that no amount of CPR was going to change that. I knew it. I thought it then. My mind screamed at me that truth. But yet, I had dialed 911 and knew that help was on the way so, in the meantime, I placed my mouth over his nose and mouth and began CPR. I did my chest compressions.

Live, damn it. Live.

In those moments, I was oddly quite calm, businesslike even, as I continued to focus on the proper breath to compressions ratio; he was going to live. I knew it. He would live.

And yet, even while I had performed CPR, I had begged and pleaded with God, to bring him back, to allow him the life that I knew that he deserved, and the one that was of greater value than mine; I wanted to make a deal to trade my life for his. The thought that somehow, in some way, I had so selfishly denied my son the right to shine, to live, because I had not been the right kind of father, was so critically apparent, that as calm as I was, I realized that my tears and mucous were covering my son's beautiful face. In my crying, which I didn't even realize that I had been doing, I thought that had I been a better person, a better father, I would not have pissed God off to the point where the death of my son was the penance and price I had to pay for my choices. But how can I feel so calm, and yet be crying so hard? This god took my son's life, who had been the good fruit of my life, and he left with me, in my life, a life wrought with the negative results of my choices and actions. A life, like so much fallen fruit, one that was rotten from the inside out, and in the death of my son, one that had been beyond repair and forgiveness.

Was I crying? Why was I crying? This makes no sense.

I can't breathe. Help me, please. I can't breathe. I can't see. I am going blind. Help me, someone, please help me.

When Malachi did not return after the torturous minutes of CPR and the prayers, the deals, the attempts at bargaining, that in a single, focused and clearly-defined moment, to this very day, that is still etched deeply in my mind, I knew that I hated God and anything that had to do with God. I knew then, in my own heart, without any questions, that there was no God of love; that religion, that church, that religious leaders were full of shit from top to bottom. That there was no life, no joy, no happiness, no recognition that I was worth a damn. I had a dead son as proof. I had another living son, who I had tried to love, as best as I knew how, that was confused and searching his father's face for answers in the moments following his brother's death. But through it all, I had a dead, infant son.

I had no answers for his older brother, who watched me, who looked at me with such confusion, and love. I had nothing left emotionally to give him. What could I have told a toddler? What could I have told myself?

I truly believe, in that moment, while I held the lifeless body of my son in my arms, waiting for the ambulance to arrive, that something deep inside went to sleep. That some part of my sanity experienced a deep and profound slumber. I didn't know how, but I knew, even then, that I would never be the same. In his death, in the knowledge that my son would never return, I understood that I was worthless. I didn't need anything else in life to more fully prove to me that I was a worthless piece of shit. In that moment, I knew that even god didn't love me.

When my son Malachi died on July 31st, 1999, he was only two and a half months old. He died. He wasn't "lost". He didn't "pass away". He died. As much as I would have liked to think that "kinder" words and phrases would have made it easier for me to digest the reality of my infant son's death, the truth is, he was dead and he wasn't coming back. No amount of precious language was going to change that for me. I had to accept what his death really was. It was final. It was complete. He was not going to return.

I cannot tell you how long it took for the ambulance to arrive. I cannot tell you what conversations I had with the medical professionals that arrived. I cannot tell you how many people arrived. In fact, were my life to depend on the answer, I couldn't even tell you what I had been wearing. There was a point, as superficial as it may sound, where I don't really remember anything. Everything was a blur. Front door opening. Front door closing. People coming in fast. People going out slow.

Men with badges, outside smoking with me. All of us crying. Police officers, I think, crying right next to me.

I knew that my son was dead. I knew that he wasn't coming back. What the hell was I going to tell my wife, his mother…

But the truth is, the thing that is crystal-clear, down to the smell of his neck, and the feel of his skin in my hands, was his death. The rest, I don't remember. I just, don't.

Over the years, I had to learn how not to let the images of his body, that would occasionally pop into my mind, drive me crazy. Early on, shortly after his death, the only way I could manage was to get drunk. I learned how to "float" through days. I was numb emotionally and psychologically, and drinking, which I knew well, was the simplest and, at least in the beginning, the most effective way to shut out the world. What I didn't know then, and what I couldn't have understood, was just how deeply removed from life I had become.

But over time, I learned, however painfully, that you cannot drink your way to peace and happiness. What sounds like commonsense to those that have never had to contend with their own hell on earth, or the emptiness that so often comes with drugs, or the guilt that can ravish one's sanity after nameless sex, is never so simple or "normal", or anything even resembling "commonsense" to those of us that have tried to keep the memories, or the pain, or the knowledge and awareness of our own sadness at bay. Or we can all try to consider the depths of hopelessness that can seem to smother someone's entire being when caught up in the endless, repetitive processes of trying to numb the pain through alcohol abuse. These are the ways and means, and not the only ones by any stretch of the imagination, that we have used. We somehow, against all hope, erroneously believed we could use these things to tamp down on the emotional suffering that we otherwise believed would destroy us. Not correct but, when one is in the midst of their own self-centered theater of pain, rational and logical thoughts are not typically crutches upon which we lean.

At some point, however one gets there, one must decide and choose, to live. To love. It's about choices and deciding. It's about making a decision, one way or the other. One decides what kind of life one wants to live, and in that realization and truth, one can no longer carry the hate, the pain, the lack of understanding and un-forgiveness to be the foundation upon which one uses to create the world one lives in. But what happens, when one experiences a life-altering trauma, is that we get stuck. We get stuck, first, in the moment itself and unless someone shows us otherwise, we then get stuck in the looping effects of the pain. Though the death is over, the rapist gone, the marriage over, we can sometimes find ourselves awash in the hurt. And in its grasp, we replay the moment, we ask the same unanswered questions, and worse than anything else, we can get trapped without even knowing it, in a place so dark that we find ourselves on a path to our destruction.

It's not that we want to necessarily die rather, we just want the pain to stop. We just want to feel alive, to feel vibrant and free of the shit that we've been carrying around, or unable to run away from. To be free of.

I think now is a perfect time to address one of the mantras that I had been taught nearly all of my life, and one that I am sure you are aware of. We are told, in one way or another, that "what doesn't kill you, only makes you stronger" and though this may be true for some, the rest of us say, bullshit. Do you really think that a man raping me as a child made me stronger? Do you think that the woman that is battered by her husband, a man that's supposed to love her, makes her stronger? Do you think, truly, that the thirteen year old transgender is made stronger by the relentless bullying they experience? Consider the parents that have to contend with the death of their children. It doesn't matter if they're two and half months old, or off serving on foreign shores in defense of this nation, do their deaths make the parents "stronger"?

But sayings like those sound good. They sound inspirational, as if they are imparting sage wisdom designed to guide and bolster your spirit as you traverse your way through the pain you encounter. What I longed for, all those many years ago, was an understanding of why I didn't feel stronger having been through what I had been through.

So like many of us, we think that we have failed, that we are too weak to rise above. We compare ourselves to others that we think have mastered the process and risen above their circumstances. We tend to think that if we are better people, that if we had that "special something", that we too, could be "stronger" for having survived the rape. The death of our loved ones. The bullying. The feeling that there is something systemically, and foundationally wrong with us. Why don't we feel stronger?

We don't feel stronger because, in my humble opinion, through what I have experienced, pain isn't designed to make us stronger. What the great and wise ones don't tell you, is that pain is a way of life letting us know that we, hurt. Sounds simple and yet, it is so deeply profound, that I missed it for years. Pain doesn't make us stronger, it gives us something in our life that needs, for the most part, to be addressed.

A broken arm does not make the arm, or the person, stronger. A broken arm, in and of itself, is just a broken arm. But for some, the pain is more intense than for others. Some experience a broken arm and shock sets in. For others, they get such an endorphin rush, that they actually laugh. My point is, not all broken arms are the same, and if you just consider the arm and the pain, nothing about the process makes the arm stronger. In fact, in that moment, and unless something is done about it, the pain will continue, and truth be told, the arm will be weaker (and perhaps, even useless).

If one gets the proper medical attention, I have been told that at the point of the break, once it heals, it's actually stronger at that point than it was prior to the break. But please note, there was proper medical attention paid to the break. It didn't heal on its own. More often than not, pain pills are used. My point isn't about the arm, it's about this myth that "that which doesn't kill you..." and the potential damage that it can do to those hurting.

I can hear some of you right now, "but Chase, there is a world of difference between a broken arm and being raped," and my response to that is, yes, there are many differences and in fact, you can't "compare" the two or the kinds of pain associated with them. But what is the same, across the board, no matter the reasons why, is that they have to effectively be dealt with for there to be healing. Sadly, there are still far too many people that believe that the healing process is a "self-correcting" or a "fix it yourself" proposition. But without being shown how to do this, or even what the tools are, most never really begin to feel the freedom that comes from their rightful peace and healing. These notions of "do it yourself" are supposed to serve as mechanisms that make one stronger. And yet for most of us, these ideas are literally, bullshit.

Someone with a broken arm, goes to see a doctor. But sadly, it is too true that some (perhaps too many) victims of rape, do not seek help. I understand that social pressures and the bullshit that's heaped upon victims in the aftermath of a rape (victim-blaming, victim-shaming, finger-pointing) prevent the vast majority from seeking help but, think on it, how did the rape make them stronger? Do you *now* see what I'm talking about?

I wasn't made stronger by the death of my son. I wasn't made stronger by the rape of my youth by the neighbor. I wasn't made stronger by the way I was raised. Argue all you want. Debate it amongst yourselves if you must, but what this book is all about is finding and accepting the freedom to evaluate your own life and deciding for yourself what is, or is not, acceptable. And that means that no one gets to decide, for me, just how much it hurt to live through the experiences that I did. My parents don't get to decide whether or not the results of my upbringing lent themselves to the successes or failures of my life. They played a part but ultimately, it took most of my life to understand that *I am the one that decides.*

So pain, or the moments that don't "kill" you, in and of themselves, don't make you "stronger". What represents the strength, over and above just surviving, is the willingness to seek out the proper ways to address the aftermath to get on a track that provides you with the peace and happiness you deserve, and is your right to experience. The "makes you stronger" part is understanding that the experience was not greater than you, and if it didn't cost you your life, it means that hope is still there. It means, in every way, that there is a chance for healing but, and here is the caveat; the healing requires a decision and action to experience the change.

This isn't about me being cold, harsh or unfeeling. And no matter how hard it may seem to grasp, I had to understand in my own life, that accepting my son's death was a critical and necessary step for me to live. To love and be loved in a way that I could understand and appreciate; I had to give myself permission to evaluate what life and love were going to mean to me. I had to understand getting past the guilt and un-forgiveness of myself, didn't mean that I loved my son any less, or that moving on was a betrayal to and of his memory.

I had to accept his death in every way that I had tried not to. I had to acknowledge it, had to accept, and more than anything else, I had to give myself permission to live the hurt. If I can share but one thing with you, it's that you must allow yourself permission to experience the whole of life. And sometimes, that means acknowledging the deepest parts of our pain. If you need help to do that, then go and get it. I am not talking about street-corner prophets with sandwich baggies, or the local liquor store. I am talking about finding someone, or something, that celebrates, in a positive way, your right to live and love. To be you.

For me, part of allowing myself the permission to finally get on with living, was to sing and to write this book. For me, and for most of my life, language and words have had a very specific and tactile meaning to me. I feel words and music the way that some people feel their favorite blanket. Having grown up in a household where words were used for a number reasons, I came to understand very early in my life, that words have power. They can have a life of their own, creating or destroying what they will but, in every way, they have life. So for me, it was absolutely necessary for *me* to use language and words that made it real in my heart and mind. Language and words made my son's death, finally, real for me. All those years that I didn't speak about it without being drunk, were years that I tried to hide. So finally, when I could first think on the words, and then put them to paper, I was slowly able to talk about him in a way that celebrated the joy of life that I had almost allowed his death to take away from me. And that, the words, made it complete in my spirit and heart.

I was finally able to say out loud, "my son, my infant little man, is dead. He's not coming back. There are no do-over's, no second chances and worse, not a damn thing that I can do about it."

How low we go into our own darkness and pain, varies from person to person but, in the time that I have been able to talk with others, I have found that each of us seeks a balance, whether we consciously know it or not, that allows us to function in the world around us, while at the same time, realizing that we hurt but not letting that pain overwhelm us. It is an ever-present, time-consuming, life-draining balancing act that many of us like to think we've mastered. I cannot speak for all but, if you are reading this book, chances are, you've realized that you want off the balance-beam, the merry-go-round and more, that it's time to live. Really live. That right now, maybe it's time to stop asking the question, "how low can you go" and ask a new one....

How high can I rise?

Chapter 3: Niggers, Cunts and Faggots

I've no doubt that most of you reading this have heard the saying, "sticks and stones may break my bones but, words will never hurt me." So, let's analyze that saying for a moment and break it down into bite-sized, easily digestible pieces. Ready?

Bullshit. There you go. That saying, and the many versions of it, are in a word, bullshit.

People that find it necessary to use those terms, and any other derogatory terms designed to demean, denigrate, humiliate and injure, are the folks that really have the problem. But because these words are usually said with some kind of false sense of personal authority and ownership, and that they are typically aimed at those that they feel are weaker, inferior and less-worthy of love, more often than not, those of us on the receiving end tend to internalize and relate to their hatred. We do this because, some part of us feels that they might be right. Some part of us, and sometimes not too deep down, believes that we deserve to be called the names, and treated so hatefully. Worse, whether they know it or not, they are generally continuing a pattern of shit that we're already living through anyway; they're just another level of confirmation.

We all react to them and their hate differently. Some of us may bark back, but typically not too energetically. Others will put on the best face possible and not allow anyone to see the utter and complete shame and devastation that we're feeling inside. But no one will know just how much it truly hurt. We won't allow anyone to see us cry. That kind of crying that makes you so tired that all you want to do when you're done crying, is take a nap. No one will see the words that we put in our journals or diaries, or on our computers, that recount just how shitty we felt. Some of us will write it all out, but then make sure that we destroy any evidence of it ever having existed. Still others will hide the evidence so that we can add the next shit-storm when it comes. We are masters at hiding our truest, deepest pain.

We have learned all the maneuvers, all of the ins and outs of hiding our anguish away, in safe, thick compartments in our hearts. But there are never enough safeguards to protect us from the next attack. We can't, especially as children, seem to find a person, place or action that protects us from further pain and worse, we don't know what the hell to do with the burden of hate and hell that we're already carrying with us. So some of us "act out". Some of us become the loner of isolation and shadows, doing everything that we can to go unnoticed. Still others will seek out ways and means of trying to fit in. Some will use sex. Some will use cigarettes. Some will resort to private cutting, eating (or not eating). Some will get high by whatever available means present themselves. Ah, but we still hurt. There aren't enough sexual partners, enough cigarettes, enough destructive actions on the planet to silence the nearly overwhelming pain that's carried around.

So we try to laugh off being called a "slut", or a "cunt", or "faggot", or "nigger", or "poor white-trash" - we learn to defend and deflect in the moment, to seek refuge and a reprieve, to just make it the hell out of there. But then the attacks come online, in relentless messages, one after another, from seemingly every conceivable angle, person and platform. We try not to answer. We try not to read, and yet we do. We do because we can't believe that it's actually happening. Why do we torment ourselves so? Why do we read them? Why can't we just laugh, shake our heads and go on about our lives, none the worse for the shit people have been saying?

Let's get real for a moment and tell the truth. If words didn't have power, why then would those filled with hate, seek first to destroy others by words? You don't often hear about fisticuffs on social media rather, you hear about a war of words, or a "he said, she said" battle of words over the internet. Words have power. The power to heal. The power to harm.

We deny ugly, offensive words. We call them the "n-word", or the "c-word" because actually using the whole word might offend someone, and in doing so, we try to minimize the meaning and intent of the use. Nigger, or Nigga' in many urban environments is often used as a greeting, or even a lyric in hip-hop music. Somehow we find a context for the use of the words, and in this context, it almost seems acceptable. Men gathered together over cold beers, may sometimes refer to women as "cunts" in anger, as a joke, and in their minds, somehow in affectionate terms? Do men, in anger, find it okay to call women "cunts", to demean, to dehumanize, to humiliate? Whatever the reason, we may never know why some choose to use words as their weapons of destruction but, that doesn't change that they do. But they are not my concern. My concern is for those who get called the names and find themselves hurting inside because of it.

Let's agree, right now, that there are those that will tell you to "just get over it", or "man-up", or "you're too emotional" and on and on. And for the purposes of this book and how I live my life, they are wrong. Period. You have to give yourself permission to decide what is or is not okay in your world. You may or may not already know that you must give yourself permission but, the challenge stems from a number of things. One, you may not know how to give yourself permission to stand up for yourself. Two, there is a great deal of fear associated with speaking up for oneself, as no one has really ever given us what we thought we needed to speak up fearlessly. Three, you may have convinced yourself that it will "pass", that it wasn't as big a "deal" as you may have thought. But if your heart is aching, and you've privately shed tears because of the pain, then admit to yourself that it does matter. That you matter.

I am not saying that the pain won't pass. I am not saying that it's a bigger "deal" than it may be but, what I am saying is critical for us to understand; if the pain lingers, won't go away, and it haunts you, then it's real and it matters. And when that happens, you have to be able to accept that it hurts and more than just understanding *why* it hurts, you need to understand *how* to begin the healing process. You deserve to know how to not let the words of others take your peace. Wait, I get it, there are those that will say, you don't understand what it's like. And that's partly true. But remember when I shared with you that we may not know the specific and individual details of everyone's pain, we can agree that there is a process that sets us free from the power that other's words can have on and to us.

I am Black. I have been called nigger, in hate, more times than I can remember. I freely confess that for years, I wondered why God made me Black, why this God put me in the dark skin that so many people seem to disdain and hate. Why would He have done this to me? How was I supposed to explain to my parents how that felt inside of me? On the few times when I did talk about it, it was a matter of logical explanations about my worth, about the historical context and a whole host of other rational gibberish that did nothing to take the sting off of having been treated in such a way to make me feel like shit. I told friends, and some of them jokingly called me a "fucking faggot". I'd laugh to try and play it off, and I learned to keep my pain to myself. Ah, wait, I was fifteen at the time, and surely I should have been mature and developed enough to not take "nigger" personally? Bullshit.

Here's a part of the process of healing. *You* get to decide what hurts you. No one else can determine for you what hurts. Not parents, not friends, not spouses, not anyone. *You* get to decide, for you. So many times, others try to explain what is or is not painful, as if their experiences and judgment somehow are more precise and accurate than our own. As a teen, far too often I was in a position where my parents thought that they knew what I was feeling and worse, whether they were aware of it or not, they had a habit of telling me *how* I should be feeling. But I had no way of telling them how much I was hurting. I had already come to believe that my father did not attend to emotions, other than anger, very well. And because of that belief, I never felt safe sharing with him how I truly felt. I learned to try and tell him what I thought he wanted to hear.

Yes, I lied. I lied because I didn't want to hear his criticisms, or his explanations of how the world worked, that had, in my mind, already been proven false. How was he to tell me how I should be feeling, when he had no idea what had happened to me that caused me to feel the way that I was feeling? How was he going to tell me how important anything was, when he didn't know the neighbor was systematically dismantling my trust? And more than that, there was always the fear that if I said the wrong thing, I'd end up on the brutal end of a belt or that fucking black paddle. Please bear in mind that there was no way that I could know what was in my father and mother's hearts and minds, so I am not professing to knowing what was in their hearts and minds. And truthfully, whether they agreed or not on the facts of those experiences, was not my concern. What was my concern, was *my* truth.

I have no doubt that the professionals will disagree with this but, what so few talk about, when it comes to words and name-calling, is that words create images in our minds. In other words, if you read the words, "elephants in cool, refreshing pools of water," what did you imagine? If you read the words, "you lazy, piece of shit," what did you imagine? My point is, I don't need to know what you actually imagined, rather, I wanted to illustrate that words create images and pictures in our minds. So, one way that I found for me to get free of the hate that had walled up inside of me, was to begin to imagine myself the way I really wanted to be and to see the life that I really wanted to live as clearly and as colorfully as I could.

This process, though seemingly easy to do, is an intricate conversation between who you believe yourself to be, and if they are separate, the identity that you express to the world around you. And can we agree, if you are still with me in this book, chances are there is a difference, however slight, between who we truly are and the masks that we allow ourselves to expose to the world around us. And that's partly why name-calling is so painful to so many of us.

All too often we carry with us, our own conversations about how worthless we feel. Though I've no doubt that each person has their own unique circumstances, I also know that we speak to ourselves about what we wish we could change about ourselves. We are masters at smiling in the face of external pains, while at the same time, we are so very adept at managing to hide the ravenous patterns of self-loathing and the fear of being discovered for who we believe ourselves to truly be; if they knew the truth about me, would they want me? And worse, we can even tell ourselves, while outwardly disagreeing with our attackers, that they may actually be right.

But, as with everything else in this book, for me, here's why it's sometimes so very, very hard to speak up, or to let the hateful words just slide past. Having been abused sexually, raped, being called a "fucking faggot" meant that I had to wonder for most of my life, in fear, if there would come that moment when someone would find out about my secrets. As irrational as I know it was, when someone called me a name, I internalized it and the name that I was being called, clashed with how I truly felt about myself. Because, as illogical as it may have seemed, the truth was, for me, that I was afraid that somehow my secret was visible to others, and if they knew about what had happened to me, then they knew just how shitty I really was. It was certainly irrational to think that but, that didn't change what was in my heart, what I knew about myself; that I had been fucked up the ass, that I had sucked a cock, that I had been some man's boy-toy. And if they knew, they would have hated me. Why, and how did I know this? Because somewhere inside of me, I had hated myself. The secrets that we keep, those are the troublesome weights about our hearts that keep us from feeling free.

As convoluted as that paragraph may have seemed and as difficult as it may have seemed to understand, that's not even what went on in my head and heart. I realize that the paragraph made little sense and that's the truth of it; *that's how I felt in my head when someone called me a name.* Everything got all jumbled up inside my thoughts and feelings, and I was unable to separate the name-calling from the lies and the truth – because I didn't know what the truth was. Not the facts regarding what had happened to me but, the truth that I was not a shitty person, or that what happened to me did not define who I was, this *truth* was not available to me at that time. So name-calling only reinforced how I already felt about myself.

That is the dirty little secret about name-calling. Name-calling, for the recipient that already *feels* shitty, is an emotional attack on a fragile state of being. It is not a rational, logical conversation that can be discussed, dissected or talked about in hushed tones. We have to be okay with acknowledging that it hurts to be called names. It has to be okay for you to know that, contrary to the wisdom of the day, it is not only okay for you to realize that it hurts but more, that once you realize it hurts, you now have the power to redirect that pain into a truth that was previously a foreign concept to you. But that takes practice. It takes being patient with yourself.

And it takes you believing, right now, that you're worth the effort. Say it with me; *I am. I am. I am worth loving. I may not believe right now but, I can be patient with myself* (and remember this, always, that if Chase believed in himself enough to write this book, that meant that he believed enough in me, to tell the truth about what he believes of me). Or, you can break it down anyway you want but, break it down and say it. You can say it out loud, to yourself silently or to yourself in the mirror. But say it – because it's true.

Say it, one more time – I am worth loving.

When we have to expend energy keeping the truth inside, it takes a toll on us. When we have to deny the truth, it means that we have to lie, and that lie gets placed upon the top of other lies, until the weight of them seems overpowering. We keep these secrets because we believe that to reveal them would cause us more pain than just keeping them to ourselves. Imagine the transgender child that knows who they are but, they are in a home where, if their parents knew the truth, that child would be out on the streets, or worse, brutalized emotionally, if not physically. And don't, for a second, think that it doesn't happen because the dirty little secret is, it happens all the time. So, instead of the child speaking the truth, for the sake of survival, they pray that they can hang on long enough to live past their home situation and then, be out on their own to live their lives as they were meant to truly live it.

Imagine the weight of that secret. Imagine, truly, how worrisome it is to keep the truth inside, when what one wants to do, is live freely with and through love. To be embraced with welcoming, compassionate arms and hearts, in a place where who you are is more than okay, but cherished, adored and loved. Imagine what that does to one's spirit, to the soul.

A transgender child, sadly, too often in our American society, is still subject to hate. Still, to this day, there are those that believe that "nigger" is a way to make a point. For our women, the word "cunt" is still used to dehumanize and humiliate. The name-calling, the verbal assaults that precede the acts of violence, are all based on words. So, in your own mind, you must give yourself the permission to stop downplaying the importance of words. Stop pretending that words are merely annoyances that can be shrugged off by simply turning one's attention to something else. As a parent, or a child, or a teen, or man, woman, Black or White, and every glorious expression of humanity that exists, we have the right to have the courage to really listen, with an open heart and mind, but more importantly, have the courage to say the words that others would use to harm us. Don't deny the ugly, hateful words. Say them. Let them roll around on your tongue until they no longer taste bitter. Take away their hate by being able to hear the word, and not bring it into your soul. You have to find a way to give yourself permission to get beyond your own puritanical understanding of the world and accept that there is a world around you that does not follow your view of it. Our children, our precious ones, are targets and words are usually the first lines of assault.

Be willing to say, "faggot", or "nigger", or "cunt", or "bitch", or any other word that a child, or you are being called, because we know, that those are the words that are used to humiliate. Say the word in and with love and understanding. Say the word with your heart and mind, as well as your lips and be willing to have an honest discussion with *yourself*. Be willing to tell the truth to *yourself*. Be willing and able to look at *yourself* and lovingly, honestly have a conversation about how fucking amazing you really are. Converse with yourself and understand that you are not the words that others would call you, or attempt to attach to you. You don't like the word? Say it but, tell yourself, truly, why you don't like the word. Acknowledge the word, and how it makes you uncomfortable but, don't deny yourself the pain, if it's there. But take away the power by taking away the connection. You are not what they say you are.

I never shared with anyone the fact that I was sexually abused. That I had been raped. And that's another thing, why do we reduce repeated rapes to something called, "sexual abuse". Sexual abuse is such a tame and watered-down term, that for me, it doesn't even begin to encapsulate the emotional and spiritual damage done to the person that's being "abused". It's not "abuse", it's rape. Plain and simple. And to make it worse, it's rape over an extended period of time. It is the literal destruction of innocence and childhood. It is a violence against the child's self-worth, the body, the soul, the spirit and everything good in them that was once untarnished and hopeful. It is not a momentary lapse in judgment for the predator, or a moment of "abuse"; it is a willful choice to destroy. And because of that, we learn to abuse drugs, alcohol, or one's body to quiet the torment that wraps itself around us, as though trying to strangle the very life out of us. "Sexual abuse" is rape. Call it what it is. Again, the power of words.

So for me, I had the double-edged challenge of being called nigger and a faggot. It didn't matter that it wasn't true. It's how I felt about myself. And it's how I felt about myself, that very nearly cost me my life.

Chapter 4: "Man-the-fuck-up, princess!"

How much of our lives are spent trying to be what others think that we should be? How much of our souls, our spirits, are spent trying to live up to definitions not of our own making?

I was born to parents that had been adults during the civil rights movement. Though my parents never really talked about their experiences, I can only imagine what they must have experienced in their lives as intelligent Blacks in a culture and world overtly struggling with racial challenges so broad and deep, as to create the Civil Rights movement. Bear in mind that, since my parents never talked to me about their experiences during that turbulent time, ever, I am merely speculating in what it must have been like but, what I do know, is that whatever they experienced and lived through must have lent itself to how they saw the world, and as a result, how they chose to raise their children. Yours truly included.

For most of my life, my definition of manhood was not of my own making. For as far back as I can recall, someone else told me what it meant to be a man. I was instructed on when it was, and was not, appropriate to cry, or to even acknowledge emotion. Those emotions that I felt, were not my own to define. I was at the mercy of others to tell me how I felt. Though I may have felt that the weather was cold, I was told that I was not. Though I felt sad, I was made to feel that I was not. That somehow, my own experiences were left for others to define and validate. It made me feel, in so many ways, that I had no voice in living my own life.

"Pick yourself up by your bootstraps", "boys don't cry" ....

"What are little boys made of?
Snips and snails, and puppy dogs tails,
That's what little boys are made of.

What are little girls made of?
Sugar and spice and all things nice,
That's what little girls are made of." - 19th century nursery rhyme

Television, movies, comics, books, neighbors, schools and the world around me determined for me what it meant to be a boy. In my own mind, whatever I believed myself to be, unless it aligned with what I was being taught, was inexorably negated by the overwhelming beliefs of others all around me.

I was not, when I was a child, a fighter. I was, in every way, a sensitive child. For me, the world was made up of bursting colors and the songs of birds. Dreams and laughter, quiet moments beneath puffy clouds and sitting quietly with a book were the things that I wanted to cling to. Football, basketball, rough and tumble, fist fights and braggadocio were not what I was built for or upon.

I was in elementary school and during story time, there were some girls that would all sit behind one another and braid each other's hair, or give one another backrubs. I know, sounds odd but, we were kids, and it was just something that we did. And though I am not sure what inspired me to do it, I joined them one day and much to my joy, I was welcomed quite easily. I was too young to understand that my friendship with females was based on the fact that I didn't confine myself to just tetherball, kickball, foursquare and running haphazardly about the schoolyard. No, for me, I was just as comfortable sitting against the wall exchanging stories with my female classmates. For me, holding hands with a girl was as natural as breathing, and more, it was merely an expression of being.

As you might imagine, once word got out that I was sitting in line with the girls braiding hair, holding hands and swapping stories, my ass was soundly kicked by several of the boys that believed themselves the arbiters of all things masculine. I was called "pussy boy", "princess", and other assorted names. This was in elementary school and was my first taste of bullying up close and personal. Did I tell my parents? Absolutely not. I knew, or at least believed, based on our family history, that sharing such disgraces were not going to go over well with my father; better to keep such masculine failures to myself.

And as much as I can go on recounting stories of my ass-beatings and the name-calling, I think that you get the idea. I know a little about being bullied and the pain that it causes. The isolation and desperation are real but, there is no language for it and worse, there is no one to trust enough to find a peaceful reprieve. Without that release, we keep the pain inside and it builds.

Even as a child, though I lacked the words to express it, I knew then, what I *felt*. If I had had the words then to say it all….

Why do people hate me so much? What is so wrong with me? Why can't they be nice to me?

What have I done that's so wrong?

Please don't hurt me anymore.

I'm sorry.

I won't do it again. But what have I done?

I hate being alive. I wish I could just go away.

"Hey, princess, where's your dress?"

I can't let them see me cry. Hide. Hide. Hide away.

Am I crying? Can they see it?

I can't breathe.

Where can I hide?

"Look at him – little pussy-boy! Maybe he wants to…"

I can't hear them. I can't hear them. I can't hear them.

I can fly. I can fly. I will not eat them, Sam I am.

"Charles," the soothing sounds of a teacher that knew. She just, knew. Open arms, no recriminations. No questions.

For a moment, I was safe to cry.

Those moments that we keep to ourselves, sharing with no others, are moments that we carry with us for far too long. Moments that we dare not share with others, out of fear. Out of a belief that no one will understand how we feel. How we've been affected by the words and the hate are uniquely our own, and very personal.

We want out of the pain. We want to be free, to be whole. To be complete in the way that we believe we're supposed to be.

But no one has actually taught us how to do that, and to blindly stumble through life seeking for peace and joy is a tiresome and frightening proposition. And though there are no promises of perfection, what we share in this book is about defining and redefining who, what and where we are. How we get there, how we choose to love and live, is our right.

Time to Kick Rocks.

Chapter 5: Can Christ be Found in Christians?

I tried reading Christian books written by several well-known leaders in the Christian religion. I tried to follow the various books and gospels to the letter. I prayed. I wept. I made list upon list. I meditated. I changed my diet. I saw "faith healers". I had hands laid upon me. I tried to pray in the "spirit". I tried baptism in water and the "spirit". I wailed, danced, sang, raised my hands to the heavens and even joined a well-known choir in Houston, Texas. In the end, the Christian "religion" didn't seem to do it for me, and worse than that, it seemed the harder I tried to just, "be", the worse the confusion and isolation got. After so much disappointment and pain, I was done chasing different "faiths", denominations, buildings, prayer groups….

But as you know, the worst of it all, is that I knew somehow, that I was the reason it wasn't working. Somehow, this Christian god had forsaken me, knowing the truth about me, the reality of my sins and the hidden nature of all that I was, he had abandoned me to a life of desperation and turmoil so rich and rife with helplessness, that I believed that I was the very definition of sin.

Point is, *for me*, religion was not the answer. I needed more than the pre-packaged answers I was given. I needed more than comments about "not having enough faith", or "God works in mysterious ways", and the one-size fits all approach to all things spiritual or earthly. It simply wasn't for me. My biggest issue with organized religion is that it tends to think that only one method works for all issues and for all people. I am not trying to deny the divinity of Christ, nor am I saying that religion is a bad thing but, for myself and many like me, there is a need within that transcends the methods that most religions wish to employ. For some of us, the pain can't be "prayed away".

For my mother and father, their Christian foundation of biblical instruction led them to believe that their form of discipline was correct, and even supported, by the religious doctrines that they chose to embrace. For them, they interpreted the tenets of their religious faith as being based, in part, on fear and blind obedience to a god that demanded nothing less than absolute fidelity to His holy word and what they believed were their scriptural parental rights and prerogatives. Again, one might think that I am against Christianity and that is simply not the case. What I am however, is a vocal opponent to any religion, cult, faith-based mumbo jumbo that believes humiliation and denigration are a means to a positive end for any person. I am opposed to any process that believes that salvation can be had turning over oneself to another, in hopes that they have an "in" to a higher being.

But sadly, too often, organized religions forsake the foundations of love, kindness and compassion, and those principles of humanity that are the best of who we are and could be, and in turn, those principles, either through ignorance or purposeful intent, get replaced by religious interpretations that fit whatever perspectives or objectives that best serve the very narrow and specific interests and purposes of *that* specific religion or leader, church or organization, regardless of how contrary to the tenets of love those objectives may actually be. From the use of the Bible to justify prohibitions against gay marriage, to others that would use the Quran as justification for killing, we find that more often than not, no matter how well-intentioned, too many religions are not generally places where freedom of expression and love and affection for *self* are generally found, accepted or encouraged; they end up creating more doubt and confusion than liberation and freedom, understanding and acceptance.

I am not suggesting that this is the case for everyone or for every church or religion, nor am I proposing that we burn down churches, mosques, synagogues or other places of worship but, for some of us, we didn't find out who we truly were (and are), by sitting in the pews, nor on the pages of the religious texts handed to us. We didn't find our freedom in the prayers of the righteous leaders, or good-hearted congregants. It is not a condemnation or indictment of religion or of those that truly believe rather, it is a sad truth that far too many of the faithful people are unwilling, or unable, to acknowledge and accept as a truth; *the answers to our deepest questions about who we are, and how to live our life with peace and happiness, are not found in religion.*

I am not negating *any* of the contributions that have been made by wonderful people in the name of their religion for humankind but, neither will I apologize for the legitimacy of my very real experiences with religion. Additionally, from those that I have coached privately, and however small that number may be, it's a quantifiable, if not heartbreaking truth, that too many people not only don't find the forgiveness, love and compassion that they deserve within the structure and hierarchy of organized religion, they find rejection, isolation and loneliness. Where there had been hope for inclusion, they instead, too often, found that the "members" were less interested in sharing love and acceptance than an ideology taught to them that they themselves didn't fully understand. In other words, conditional love and a focus on membership in the "faith" took the place of understanding and compassion.

I can already hear the devout, the faithful, the fundamentalists and the pious preparing to debate the comments that I've made, and that's okay. In fact, it's to be expected. But that certainly won't change my experiences.

My mother and father were not evil people; they did what they believed should be done, in hopes that their actions would result in a life for me that they believed that I should have. They were, in their own way, doing the best that they could, believing that they were doing the right thing, in the right way, at the right time. I don't fault them for that. I don't. They had no way of knowing, in those days of corporal punishment, of joyful hopefulness, just how negatively their "hopes" would impact my life. And for those of you that might be tempted to think that I am blaming my life choices on mommy and daddy not loving me enough, or the "right way", that is not the case. More on that later. Suffice it to say, that for me, religion and discipline were not the only aspects of my childhood to inspire this book.

No matter what you may be thinking about my relationship to and with religion, this book is not about religion. As I'm sure you have already gathered, I don't really believe in organized religion, or any inherently limiting doctrines or misguided theologies (or any person or organization for that matter) that do little in the way of teaching the steps needed to live one's most right and authentic life. For example, I believe that the stories in the bible are there to illustrate specific points about the nature of who we really are, and that most organized religion do very little in the way of shedding light on the steps, or processes, if you will, on how to accomplish, succeed at and ultimately, live the life we are created to live.

So yes, religion does wonders in creating the "feel-good" moments that so many are accustomed to and yet, when the "feel-good" has faded, what remains? When the "amens" and "hallelujahs" are over, what's left? I am not here to condemn your religious beliefs, or to assert that all religion is bad. Rather, what I am saying is this, for me, and this is a foundational principle upon which this book was written; church was never the intended purpose of Christ. And since church was never the intent, my understanding of who I am, what love is and what my life should be should never have been predicated on religion and the narrowness of a specific interpretation.

Too often, contemporary religion seems to merely entertain, or to make one just "feel good". I truly believe that for most, church was originally, at best, to have been a place of empowerment, of spiritual, soul-ish, and physical liberation. Instead, it seems to be an escape from the world that we live in. Even if can believe that, in every way, church was intended to teach, to extol, to express the manners and methods of Christ, so that each member of the body of Christ, or the church as a whole, might also express, extol and live life as Christ had intended for us to live, we have failed. So again, whatever your religious affiliation, that is your own personal path, and one that I respect for you.

Though I believe in the teachings of Christ, and I will, in some instances, use the bible as my foundational texts for certain assertions and points, this is not about cramming religion down anyone's throat (as I will also reference other religious texts along the way) nor is this a "Christian" book; don't get it confused with the religious writings of the church leaders that write one book after another. This book is not one of those. Because, for me, in the end, had I not been exposed to Taoism, Islam, Buddhism and other thoughts and beliefs outside of mainstream religions along the way, I could not have, nor would I have, come to the understanding that I have now. So, if your doctrine or religion, to you, is the only correct means of understanding life and yet you're not living the life that you know and believe you should be living, then perhaps you've come to this book at the right time.

Got it? So, in a nutshell, do with religion what you desire. And like everything else in this book (and life), allow yourself to ask the questions that you feel you need to ask. Let no one dissuade you from taking the path that you need for your absolute freedom. Take the ideas, guidance, advice, experiences and thoughts of others on your own terms. No person, no matter how righteous they may claim to be, has the right or authority to determine who you are. I am not talking about legality or law. I am talking about someone telling you what you need to do, or have to do, or should do. That includes me. When you see something italicized, it's because it means, or meant, something to me and in that, I want to make sure that I share it in a way that emphasizes a matter that I believe can be considered something worth not only sharing, but of your consideration. But even with that, I am *not* telling you *who you are*.

That is for you, and you alone, to determine.

Ultimately, like diets, it behooves you to look beneath and beyond the euphemisms and rhetoric to discern what is going to work for you.

For the Christian that would seek to instruct, that would otherwise profess and speak of a great love, Jesus taught that to love, is to act. It is so much more than words. And yet, so few Christians, at least in my limited experience, truly embody the nature of forgiveness, compassion and a willingness to see in others, that which they claim to have in abundance. Love.

36 "Teacher, which is the greatest commandment in the Law?" 37 And Jesus replied to him, "'YOU SHALL LOVE THE LORD YOUR GOD WITH ALL YOUR HEART, AND WITH ALL YOUR SOUL, AND WITH ALL YOUR MIND.' 38 This is the first and greatest commandment. 39 The second is like it, 'YOU SHALL LOVE YOUR NEIGHBOR AS YOURSELF [that is, unselfishly seek the best or higher good for others].' 40 The whole Law and the [writings of the] Prophets depend on these two commandments." – Matthew 22:36-40 Amplified Bible (AMP)

And for those righteous few, that would seek out verses to pummel, humiliate and denigrate others, I believe that they have failed to read through the entirety of the words of their prophets, who taught…

34 But the stranger who resides with you shall be to you like someone native-born among you; and you shall love him as yourself, for you were strangers in the land of Egypt; I am the LORD your God. - Leviticus 19:34

It is so very, very easy to pick and choose the verses that support a given belief and yet, why do so few pick the foundational principle of loving others as they love themselves? Could it be, that beyond all of the rhetoric and impassioned fervor for their faith, that they lack an understanding of what true love is? Love never seeks to injure….

Admonishments to love. Love. And, love some more. From that foundation was to have flowed all the best of humankind. And again, not as an indictment of a person or religion, you, dear reader, must take upon yourself the accountability and mantle of seeking truth in a love that is true. And it starts with loving yourself.

It all starts with, loving you. Just as you are. This very moment. Yes, right now. Right here. Right where you find yourself on the journey of life. Love. You.

"But Chase, you sound so anti-Christian. You sound like someone that had a few bad experiences and then you lumped all Christians into the same category. There are some truly wonderful Christians. People that would give their lives for others…."

Let me address this directly and forthrightly. If you have garnered anything about me at this point, it should be that I recognize generalities and stereotypes. I also acknowledge that my experiences are not everyone else's. Couple that with the fact that I even said, this is not about all "Christians" rather, this is about the fullness of my experiences and the well-intentioned people that were a part of my life. So, if you need to discard this book, or be angry with me because I am not a fan of organized religion, like everything else about me and this book, that's okay for you to not like it, or me. But now, I want to speak in broad, vague terms that I know many will not understand. These are more of *my* words. My reflections. My understandings. My truths.

I read in the bible about how much this god loved me, and yet, when he got pissed off enough, he destroyed all of humankind, to euphemistically start from scratch. I read about a "loving" god that required someone to make a sacrifice of someone they loved, in order to prove their obedience and fidelity. I was taught about a god that I was supposed to fear. A god that was a "jealous god", and that in his own words, "vengeance" was his. More than anything else, you have a god that would kick you out of the house if you ate shit that wasn't yours, or if you married into the wrong tribe, or copulated with someone other than a close relative. Wait, that may have been a misunderstanding – I get the whole Noah and Abraham, and Moses thing all confused.

We also have a god that has a "chosen" people, and those not of his chosen "people", are subject to plagues, locusts and the deaths of their first born. And if that wasn't enough, men thought that to expand his righteous cause, they would create the "crusades", in the name of their "god". Crusades that arguably, killed more people in the name of god than the Black Plague itself, and even that was supposed to represent god's punishment on a misbehaving people.

And for every one of you religious instructors, preachers, pastors and theologians, let me spare you from having to save me.

I believe in the teachings of Christ. I do. But there is nothing you can tell me about the anger of your god that is going to change the following…. There are no prayers you can extend, or crackers, or wafers, or juice, wine or conversations in a box that can replace the truth of my experiences. I accept them. I own them.

The Christ I love and know, is a little something like this….

When you get caught in the act of adultery, as in busted, in the act, butt-ass naked, with witnesses to see the whole show, this Christ that I know, well, he forgives. He doesn't ask for a play-by-play, or details – he just forgives. And more than that, the people causing all the shit, the ones that want to do all the damage, are told, "let you, who is without sin, cast the first stone." Which in contemporary terms means, unless you're perfect, you're in no position to bring anyone before a cause for judgment. I can go further, I promise you but, this is not a case of right or wrong, rather, this is about an example of how the Christ in "Christian" seeks first to forgive.

"Okay, Chase… does that mean I'm supposed to forgive my rapist/attacker/father/mother/brother/fill-in-the-blank after all that they've done to me?" Short answer, yes. Let me explain why.

Suppose that two people are caught in the act of adultery – bear with me, please – and in this scenario, that only means that at least one person in the act was married, right? Suppose that the man was married and that he was raping the woman. We have been told that, in this story, the woman was the "harlot" – but in this example, I submit, that she's being raped by a married man but, legally, that's still adultery (and yes, check the law – I don't make this up).

And now, who is Christ talking to? Who is being forgiven and more, *what* is being forgiven? What if what he was forgiving is the way we feel about ourselves? What if he was talking about the sin of not "loving ourselves"?

But more than anything else in that story, what if the sin he was referring to, was the sin of not letting him love you?

Step away from Christ and Christendom and ask yourself this one question; did anything in the questions that I asked myself, help you in any way? If yes, then great! If not, then great!

What the fuck?

There is no wrong answer. Not trying to be all mystic. Here's my point.

You have earned the right to ask your own questions. You have earned the right to seek your own truth.

You have earned the fuckin' right to be you.

You will, my dear reader, my partner, learn and understand soon enough, that I am in no position to judge anyone else. But by the same token, I am also not someone that needs another to define who I am, who I have become, or who I may be.

So, let me get back to the "love" part….

"I am broken. I am not the one that you want to love. I am not the one that you remember. I am not the poetry that you want to share. I am not the song you want to sing. I am no more, the one you want to remember.

What I need, what I seek to find, what I want you to know, is the one that I am now.

How do I stand in life, and breathe in hope, when you do not see who I am in this moment? How do we, how do I, come to live again?

I am broken.

Can you love me, still?"

In my own life, I await the day when the admonishment to "…love your neighbor, as you love yourself…" becomes the mantra to which all "Christians" adhere and pledge.

Until then, I hope. I dream. And work on my little book.

And love the misfits….

Nothing about this is an indictment on the Christian masses rather, this is about my experience. I expect that you have your own views and that's the way it's supposed to be.

For the record, this little meandering section was all about how difficult it was to get my own thinking straight. There was so much about me that I didn't understand, including the things that ran through my head. My thoughts didn't seem to belong to me. As rambling and confusing as it may have seemed for you to read and understand, imagine, for just a moment, how a child of thirteen felt trying to piece together the loneliness and emotional emptiness that washed over him. If I could go back and hold that child, I would. But I cannot go back.

I can write this book and share it with you. I can share a truth of how that child became a man that learned how to breathe again. I can share how that child grew into someone that, despite what others said and believed of him, learned that love is not about violence, deprivation, deceit and pain. What I share in this book, is not just about me, or only my life but rather, I share this as a willing and vocal member of a club that should never be but sadly, is; we are the ones that have been mistreated, berated, belittled, abused, fucked-over, shit-upon....

But we survived.

And now we thrive.

In the end though, for those that would pray for my soul, or my life in the hereafter, I ask, do you live and express the truth of Christ, or do you find it more socially expedient to talk the talk, rather than walk the walk?

"Love your neighbor, as you love yourself."

As you *love* yourself.

Your. Self.

Chapter 6: The Truth in Hope

I can never go back and change what has already happened in your life. As much as I would like to heal whatever wounds you may have suffered, I cannot. I cannot undo your choices, my choices, or the choices of others that have crossed your path along your journey of life and love. But if you will allow me a moment, I would like to finally, say what I was previously too afraid to say.

For what I knew of love, in my broken and faulty understanding, I have loved you since your first breath. I have longed to find ways to escape my own fears and trepidation about life, to express to you just how much I do love you. But I wasn't able, and for that I am so deeply, and so profoundly sorry.

It was never my intention that you should ever question your worth for anything that I may have said or done. Or worse, for what I didn't do. For all those things that I didn't say, for every moment that I didn't embrace you. I am sorry.

It is my hope that you can forgive me. And if I have erred in believing that I have ever even crossed your mind, I apologize for having been presumptuous.

I accept that I failed in those moments, when the chance was present, to acknowledge my own sense of "self" and in turn, I failed to be an example of what love is, and should ever be.

So with hope, know that I have grown to understand the power of words. And now that I understand, I can freely say, with every fabric of my being, and with the breath that is life;

I love you.

Now, bear with me for just a moment longer....

I have cried all I'm ever going to cry for feeling like shit over what others say about me, or more, even think about me. I have reached a place where you and I can have some coffee and conversation, and leave the table and hug one another with the deepest love.

I appreciate you. I know your shadows and the angry darkness that haunts your waking hours. Not enough laughter. Not enough time in the day, or miles on the earth for us to run and hide. Together, we stop running. We stop, right now.

Right now, you get to claim your freedom from every voice in your head and heart that would convince you that you don't deserve being loved for the beautiful and wonderful gift of *and to* life that you are.

You are not a mistake. I don't care what you may hear from the world outside, or the voice in your own mind – you were graciously and wondrously created. Whatever failures you may have encountered, whatever hell you may have endured, it was not of your doing. As you are reading this, hear my voice. I know, weird right? But hear me anyway. Imagine, if you have to, and listen to every word that I am sharing.

We are not fuckups. We are not worthless. We are not lost, losers, refuse to be discarded.

We are, you and I, survivors and overcomers of the highest order. Think about the strength that it took for you and I to get to this moment in time, right now, after all that we've been through. Do you really, really believe that a coward makes it this far? No. No. And no a thousand times.

We, you and I, have seen the worst that there was to see and we're still standing baby. Yep, here we are, in this moment together, to remind one another just how amazing we are.

Whatever the world would have us believe about ourselves, whatever voices would seem to convince us that our lives are empty and need to end, well, we now get to remind one another that we are, fucking amazing.

That's right, go ahead and smile. You know that I'm telling you the truth.

The rapist didn't win. The pedophile didn't win. The bully didn't win. The ignorance and hatred of the world didn't win.

We are, here. You and I.

Together.

For those of you that are reading this and questioning, that are still having a hard time grasping the truth that I am sharing, I get it. I do. And there is no judgment here. I have been there.

I have questioned my own worth to the point that I tried to end my own life (November 2, 1994), and yet, here I am. All of the ugliness, the shit, the darkness – it almost got me – but it didn't. And by all that is right and good, you are still *here*. The seed has been planted.

Let no one tell you that you're still here out of cowardice or that you're too weak. Again, I say, think about it – think about you and the strength in you to still stand. However weak you may feel, or felt in the past, recognize, if even for the first time, that it takes an amazing person to still stand after what you've been through. No one, and I mean *no one*, can take away from you, the knowledge of what you, and you alone, have experienced. No one, from this moment forward, can ever again deny your truth. No one, from this day forward, gets to define, for you, who you are, who you were, and who you shall be.

And, dear reader, if you still question, if you still hear the voice of doubt, that's okay. Understand that for some of us, it took some time for us to believe the shit (the *shit* being whatever you believe about yourself that makes you think you're undeserving of real, true and unconditional love) and, in truth, it may take some time for you to get used to the "new" voice in your head. But listen to it. Listen to your heart.

It may be a frightening prospect. There may come times when you find yourself afraid and lonely. You may wonder if what I have shared is true. You may discover that, during the revelation, it seems that everything is falling apart. But if you can believe in you, and in the truth of your beauty and wonder, you will come to live the fullness of love and life that you so richly deserve.

I cannot convince you of anything. I cannot force you to see. And in truth, I would never, ever try and decide for you what is right for you.

But if you and I get to have some coffee, you may have to contend with me giving you a hug.

And telling you I love you.

Chapter 7: The "Beginning"

Yoga. Guided meditation. Running. Music. Prayer. Alcohol. Drugs. Sex. Religion. And the list of ways that some people try to connect with themselves and their own truth, goes on and on. For me, I have tried the sex, the alcohol, the drugs, the meditation, the yoga, prayer, music, religion… and in the end, in that moment, I found my truest beginning.

The Beginning, was in allowing myself the right to love, me. I had to learn what love was to and for me. I had to learn what it meant to be patient with myself, to offer forgiveness to myself. In a world that seemed, at times, hell-bent on my destruction, I was finally able to allow myself a moment to reflect on what it all meant to me. In that reflection, I had to make some hard choices and accept that, in the end, in so many ways, I didn't really know what love was.

I had to define, quite clearly, what it meant to love, to be loved and in return, to love another. With each step, a new and finer understanding took place. It wasn't always pleasant, and the world didn't magically become perfect simply because I decided to love me on my terms. I still had legal issues to contend with. I still had child support payments, bills to pay, money to make but, there was something new.

I had hope that wasn't based on a false sense of needing others to validate me. For the first time, I had a hope that meant, my beginning, was on my terms.

I understood, finally, what it meant to tell my fears, my doubts, other people and their opinions, thoughts and ideas about who I was or should be, to lovingly, respectfully, Kick Rocks.

Be Real. Be as honest as you can with yourself. Take some time during your day to just *listen to yourself. Listen to your thoughts, that voice in you that has tried to convince you that you are not worth loving.* Don't argue with yourself. Don't wrestle with it, just observe what you're saying, what others have said, and when the time comes, simply remind yourself that yes, that may have been true but, thankfully, you've now forgiven yourself and you're allowing yourself to create your truest happiness. There is no magic trick to this. It will probably take some time. How long, I don't know, but I do know, like any other conversation you have, some go easier than others. But the key here is to Be Real. Tell the truth. Allow yourself to finally say that if it hurt, it fucking hurt. No need to deny your truth. No need to be the hero on the outside, or the shrunken wall-flower any longer. Or anything else that you've accepted as truth that opposes who you really are. If you need to take out a pad and paper and write it down, then do so. Let me share with you an example.

Who decided that I was a nigger? Who was given the power to decide, that because of the color of my skin, that I was a nigger? And really, what does nigger mean anyway? Who decided that? And more, why did someone else's view of me mean that it was somehow true? Okay, so I have darker skin than some, and yet, lighter than others. So, someone, with whom I've never met, conversed, or otherwise had any dealings with, decided that an entire group of people, were now going to be Niggers. And further, that nigger was a bad thing, something to be feared, or loathed, or humiliated or anything else not of my choosing. Someone made a decision, and I was supposed to accept that decision as fact. Why?

I am *not* talking about racism as a whole, or the Civil Rights Movement, or the validity or foolishness of a particular social construct. What I am talking about, is deciding for me, what and who I am. What I learned, was to ask questions and then decide for me, what applies to me, and what doesn't. I cannot change the mind or heart of the person that believes that Blacks are this, or that, or how we, I, should live but, more importantly, it's not my job to change the hearts and minds of those that did not ask to have their hearts and minds changed. And there's a great deal of freedom in knowing that I love people enough to allow them to live their lives as they see fit.

It doesn't mean that I appreciate the word being hurled about but, I am no longer subject to the pain that it once caused me. I am no longer a person that needs to ask why they called me a name, or wonder why, there are those that believe as they do. I get to go about my life knowing that not everyone is going to like me, and that's okay. It also means that I am free to just be me. To Be Real.

By finally stopping and taking time to really understand why nigger bothered me so much, I was able to understand that though it's not necessarily pleasant, the word was given the power to injure me, *by me*. Meaning, how I interpreted the word, how I allowed it to affect my peace, was the key. If I didn't identify with their ugliness, if I knew who I was, then did it matter what someone else said? No more than we can stop gossip, can we stop someone from believing what they truly believe. No amount of legislation is necessarily going to change someone's heart. Perhaps they may not openly spew the words (and for some, that's enough) but, they may still harbor a great dislike. My point is, you are not going to change someone's mind by trying to convince them of your worth.

And here's the worst/best part about it all. They called me nigger, and it hurt my feelings. I had given over my power to someone else, because of a word. Think on that for a moment. If they had called me short, or tall, or thin, or fat, or smart, or stupid, or anything else, if I know that I am not those things, then more often than not, I can just roll my eyes and go about my business. But yet, that word nigger, which was still only a word, no matter the historical context, no matter how often it was used to harm, humiliate and denigrate, was still, at its core, just a word. Just like the word "short", it was only a word. I had finally learned, that *I* get to decide what they mean for me.

Granted, we can debate the merits of words and their impact. We can discuss the value of collective acceptance as it relates to culture and its norms. But my point here, is that when a word makes you feel anything less than your best, then it's on you to examine why and what you can do to take away that power. The freedom is knowing that you, not them, have the power to determine the value.

Being Real means that you no longer just allow old ways to go on haphazardly in your mind and heart. Being Real means that you are willing and able to evaluate, on your own terms, those things that once caused (or may still cause) you distress. It takes practice. It does. No point in lying about it. But consider how long it took for others to convince you of who you think you are now. Consider, that though it took a while for me to get it, it didn't take a lifetime. Trust yourself.

But how do you do this? What are the steps? What are the 1-2-3's, and the a-b-c's of the process? What's the secret?

Though I know, as with just about everything else in life, that there are those who will disagree with what I am about to say regarding the process, it doesn't change what I believe to be the truth. But, here it is:

Ask yourself what you really want. Not what you kinda want, or what you could take or leave but, what you truly desire, those secret desires that are kept in those places, kept all to yourself. Those wants and needs so completely you, that they are kept where no one can come in and destroy all that they mean to you. No, no, no – don't shrink back from the truth. Ask yourself what it is that moves you as nothing else has, or can, and that reflects the truest essence of who, what and why you are, *on your terms*. Being real with yourself, about yourself, as frightening as it may seem in the moment, is the first crucial step. And for the record, as I promised, this step, for me, nearly made me give up on pursuing the life I really wanted. I did not enjoy the emotional fallout that came from doing a personal inventory and then having to decide what about me stayed, and what about me had to go.

The whole process, like everything else in our lives, that sadly, no one really tells us, or instructs us on, is not an easy one. It requires a truth and honesty that many of us have not tended to exercise with ourselves. I am not talking about the shit we think of ourselves, or the ugly things that we say to ourselves. Nor am I referring to the insidious lies that we've clung to over the years, that keep us mired in near hopelessness. No, I am talking about, referring to, and speaking on a truth that we've either not acknowledged, or have been too afraid to believe could ever be a part of who we think we are, or dare dream to be.

Chances are that you're expending a lot of energy fighting what it is that you truly want. You might have convinced yourself that what you're doing is moving towards what you desire, but the truth is, *you are more than likely actively moving away from what you really, really want. You may be telling yourself that you're heading towards your future, when in part, you are running or hiding from the truth of who you are.* You might believe that moving towards that education, to get that great job, is going to provide you with the great life so that you can finally do what it is that you really want to do. And for some, that may be true. But for you, you have to truly analyze what *that* is, for you.

So much of the stress we feel is founded in the notion and actions that we think that we need to take, that don't truly lend themselves to the fulfillment of who we/you truly are. Hard work, knowledge, a great education, the right contacts and social standing mean nothing, if they don't fulfill the deepest understanding of who you truly are.

Considering where you are in life, and how open you've been to yourself, you may already know what it is that you truly, really want. But you've wrestled with how to make it come to pass. And now, here's the secret; you cannot, any more than you can force some to love you, control how life is going to present itself to you. Your purpose is to clearly define who you are and what you truly desire, and the world, the universe, god, life, whatever you desire to call it, takes care of the details. I know, I know – it all sounds like some hokey bullshit but, ask yourself this, when was the last time you experienced joy beyond description? When, and if, you can pinpoint it, then ask yourself if it was something that you truly desired and then, as best you can, try and figure out how life put all the pieces together to bring you that moment and you'll quickly see, that other than the deepest desire, there was little that you could do, or did, to bring it all to pass. Not my rules. It's just how it is.

Stop fighting yourself and allow yourself to believe in *your* truth.

Be Free. It is my personal belief that you can't be free, until you get real. So long as the opposing thoughts and beliefs dominate your life, you are still a prisoner, as it were, to circumstances, opinions and ideas beyond your control. But more importantly than the outside factors, are the very real beliefs that you keep about yourself, within yourself. Those voices, those conversations and beliefs that we keep within ourselves have perhaps more impact than the experiences that we've had. What I mean is that the experience is gone, as in the rape is physically over, but the memory and the beliefs of what it all meant emotionally, the conversations in our own heads about our own worth and the ideas about rape, continue.

I will take it a step further and say, if we are waiting for someone to apologize for us to have closure, who then actually has the power in that equation?

It is possible that an apology or an explanation will give you the impression that it was the closure that you were looking for. But that simply isn't the case. Again, if you are looking outward for the validation of your freedom by and through someone other than yourself, then you will continue to need someone else's permission and authority to be happy and peaceful. Even though we've been taught a certain way of doing things, it doesn't necessarily mean it's correct. Let me share two examples with you. One of a social nature, and the other of a very personal perspective that helped shape the way I relate to the world around me.

A certain well-known celebrity posted a selfie on a social-media platform. This was not the first time, and yet the response from several other well-known celebrities was swift and cutting. The comments weren't in any way kind to the original poster. But here's the interesting thing; it is so easy for celebrities to talk about the dangers and evils of bullying and yet, they allow themselves to engage in that very same behavior, and their justification is that they are "calling it as it is". Ultimately, the original poster defended the images and the right to post them as they saw fit. There were some tense exchanges between the opposing parties, and finally other celebrities entered the fray in defense of the original poster. But let's take a brief look at this for a moment.

First and foremost, from my perspective, people spend entirely too much time judging others and creating standards that they wish to impose on others rather than attending to their own lives. Their actions and words are read or seen by others and somehow, it's missed that the messages they're sending out can cause others to question their own self-worth. Who wants to be judged? Who really wants to be the target of others, simply because of how you see the world? But we give celebrities a pass on their bad behavior, while at the same time holding them up as examples to emulate. Why did the original poster give a rat's-ass what others thought in the first place?

Think of a particular celebrity and her willingness to take on "slut-shaming" head-on by being who she is, and by not shrinking back from the attacks on her character and personal choices. Doesn't matter if you agree with her stance, her attire, her attitude or the manner in which she has chosen to address the issue. The point is, she is claiming her right to be her, by defining for herself, and for others, that their bodies and their choices are their own. And anyone that doesn't like it, well, can kiss their asses. In Chapter 3 we dealt with name-calling, and here is a prime example of redefining, re-purposing a word that was originally meant to harm and humiliate. Own it. Take the power away. Be Free. No one gets to define you.

But Chase, it's easier said than done. Okay. Yes and no. Yes, it's easier to keep doing things the way that you've always done them, and in turn, it means that you won't go beyond that level of discomfort. And no, because sometimes it's a trial in itself just to address what it is that hurts, and that, as frightening as it may appear, is an integral part of the process.

If you want to be free, you have to live freely. You begin in your heart and mind. You first find that freedom in your self-talk, in the conversations that you have with yourself all the time. Be Real about it, and then, when the opportunity presents itself, and it will, allow yourself, even through the fear, to take that moment and Be Free.

To close this section out, I want to share a personal experience and why apologies don't have the power that you think they do.

I will never see the man that raped me ever again, except in my imagination. There will be no apologies. But for a great deal of my life, I allowed those moments to cloud, to cast a shadow over my sense of self. My sexuality was a question to me. My self-worth was paper-thin, and subject to being easily hurt by words that others never gave a second thought to. There were times when I dreamed of asking him "why". There were many, many nights when I imagined him explaining why he'd raped me. Every sentence, every word, every emotion was crystal-clear in my mind in how I wanted to hear him explain and apologize for doing what he'd done to me. Life never afforded me that opportunity and because of that, I thought that I needed to end it all on November 2nd, 1994. Certainly there were other issues but, the rape was in the top three of my reasons to be done with life.

What I didn't understand at the time, was that every time I imagined the conversation with him, I relived the shit that he did to me. Imagine how messed up that was; here I was trying to be free and yet, the very idea of him caused me to literally, in my mind, relive those very moments over and over and over again. I didn't know that what I wanted was to be whole. I didn't have the vernacular to express that what I truly wanted was to not hurt any longer. I wanted to be able to have sex with someone and not feel guilt and shame crash down on top of me like every shitty feeling I'd ever had. No one told me how to be free. To be, free. For good.

I cannot speak for you and perhaps you truly believe that an explanation or apology will be the thing that helps you come to terms, or get some closure, or set something free within you that somehow this other person holds the key to. But if you can trust me, just a bit, then let me suggest that you take that pen and pad, and look over it again. Look at what it is that you really want. Do you want an explanation and/or apology from someone that you believed wronged you, or is the truth that what you truly want, is to be free of the pain and loneliness, the emptiness and longing so much a part of your world that you've lived for so long? Do you really want to confront the person, or do you just want to finally be free of them, and what they did, so that you can move on with your life and be whole, complete and deeply, wondrously happy? In other words, decide if the confrontation, or apology, or something else that *they* can do is the key to your happiness. Or can you let it go, forgive and move on, taking back your strength and peace? This is not to suggest that you set aside legal avenues that might be applicable rather, I am referring to being stuck in a cycle wherein they have the power to keep you mired in a past action.

For so long, we have been told about closure and for me, I was unable to pursue legal avenues and as a result, feeling that I was powerless, I was stuck with the nightmares, the drinking problems and other issues, until I was able to let it go. It doesn't mean that I have forgotten, nor does it mean that I think what he did was right. It simply means that I no longer wanted to be a prisoner to the memories, and that meant that I had to decide what closure was going to be for me. If it's an apology, or some other external means that you need, then do what you feel you must do to be free.

And here's the other aspect that was already touched on; you cannot control others. What if you do get a chance to confront this person, and they tell you to "fuck off", then what do you do? Are you forever a prisoner? What if they're dead? What if they simply don't know why they did what they did? What answer(s) will ever be enough? How many tears do they have to shed, and what if after you leave, they are laughing their asses off behind your back? What does it all mean? Again, if you can, consider a different route.

Why not take the opportunity to reclaim your freedom, through *your* own power, right now? This moment is yours to do with as you desire. Sure, you can seek out revenge, or closure, or hope to get your freedom back from someone else but, I submit, that you have the power, this very moment, and more, the right to claim yourself free. You won't necessarily "feel" free the moment the decision is made, and sadly, too often, when people don't feel an immediate rush of change, they give up. Remember to be patient with yourself. It took some time to feel the way that you do now, and it may take some time to get used to the new way of life. But it is your right to be as happy as you desire to be.

It is not up to someone else to apologize or explain the reasons for what happened – it is your time, right now, to let it go. Reimagine the life that you truly desire. Forget how you think they should apologize. Let go of the images of revenge. Stop, right now, and see yourself as you really, *really want to be*. And here's some shocking stuff for you to contemplate; how much more peace will you know, if you allow yourself to spend some time with the truly wonderful you that you are. See it in your mind and heart. Learn what love is to you, define it, shape it – own it. And then, let it course through you as you deserve. Yes, Be Free.

In the end, when we seek for justice, or closure, or reason, in so many ways, we've given up our power to "be", ourselves. We have allowed something external to us, to determine the "when", the "how" and the "why" of our peace of mind. Again, I am not suggesting that if you truly believe that you "need" something from someone else, that you should let that go however, for me, in every way, there was nothing that my father or the "rapist" could do or say that was going to give me the true peace and freedom that I deserved.

I realize that what I say here goes against some very conventional wisdom and more, there are many, many people that have shared their path to "freedom" and closure by having someone explain "why" they did what they did, or answer all of the questions they asked, or apologize, or something else that was designed to set them free.

I love my father. I love my mother. They may not see their child-rearing as being anything other than a positive. And this is not about being rational or logical. In every way that matters, it has to do with their right to choose for themselves what they believe. So, if that's the case, what apology could they ever offer? If they don't believe that they've erred, why should they apologize? Perhaps I can share with them how I see it, how it all affected me, how I think and feel that I should have been raised? Or, I could have decided that I was done looking back at what "could have been", or "should have been", or how it could have been different. Instead, there was a choice to get free. There was a decision that I wanted to be free.

A choice. A decision.

As frightening as all of it was, it was necessary for me to relinquish the old ways of relating to the world. I had to let go of the notion that my parents, or the "rapist" was ever going to come around to my way of thinking, or have a moment of positive consciousness and determine, for themselves, that there was another choice that they could have made and within this discovery, that somehow, they owed me an apology. That through it all, I could wait and hope for them to realize that I was deserving of their apology and more, that they would come to the conclusion that they needed my forgiveness. But that didn't happen.

May never happen.

I no longer care.

And that's the beauty of letting it go. I didn't need their apology. I didn't need their permission to get on with truly living. That somehow, in the letting go, I was able to get beyond all of the drunken, tear-filled nights of loneliness and feelings of worthlessness. I am not talking about just "not drinking". Nope.

In the letting go, I found out what it was to feel, deep inside, a release that was, in many ways, so foreign and unknown, that I nearly decided that it would be easier to stay drunk. I know that sounds odd but, I was so accustomed to having lived in a state of pain, that when it was gone, I had an "oh shit" moment, when it occurred to me that I was going to have to live in ways that I had never experienced. But along with that, there was hope. I mean it. There was hope that not only could I do it, this live and experience life anew but more, I was actually excited to discover how it was all going to pan out.

And that's another unexpected gift of letting it go; somewhere in the process, you stop trying to control other people. You let go of the expectations that people need to, or should do, what *we* think or believe that they need to, or should do. In other words, we let go of the belief that our judgments, or needs, or wants, are somehow their responsibility. We allow them to live their lives and in return, we find that we are free to experience life without the burden of being disappointed or wounded when they fail to meet our expectations. It doesn't mean that we're going to allow people to mistreat us rather, it simply means that if they don't acknowledge us, or apologize, that our lives are no longer dependent upon those things happening and more, in our freedom, we find that there is more room in our hearts and souls to experience more joy. Because in the letting go, we release the hate, the pain, the fear, the anger, the feelings of loss and in the process, there is then, after letting it all go, space for all the joy and wonder that life is so willing to grant us.

We reclaim our "selves". We are free to set ourselves onto a path of our own choosing. One with more joy. More freedom. More hope.

For ourselves. For others that we love.

Be Free.

In the next section, we wrap it up. But before we move to the next section, I want you to consider, as I had to do, what it would mean to you, (I mean *really mean to you*) to be free of the need to have someone else dictate your closure, or your freedom, or your right to live and love. Close your eyes, and even if only for a brief moment, see what life would be like without that weight. Feel what it would be like to walk a path of your own choosing.

Let's move on....

Chapter 8: A Taste of Freedom

It doesn't happen overnight, for most of us, that we realize that we are so much more than what others have told us we were. And for most of us, we have our own inner voice reminding us that we are not worth the time of day. So we go about our lives, doing the best we can, telling ourselves that "this is how it's supposed to be". We do an excellent job of convincing ourselves that the negative stuff we hear, or that we tell ourselves, is the truth. We may see an image of what a woman is supposed to look like, or the kind of car that a man is supposed to drive. What size, how far, how much, when, where, and on and on and on, we are deluged with information and ideas about who we're supposed to be.

I am Black. So that meant that I knew my place in the world. Because someone explained that to me. I knew that I was going to have to wear suits and ties to be respected, because someone told me that this is how successful people dressed. I knew that I was going to have to live in a certain part of town, with the right car, the appropriate job and the "just right" body – because all of my life, people had been defining things for me. Oh, you and I both know that the pressures and stressors of fitting in can be, and in many ways are, a real pain in the ass. Now, if you have convinced yourself that your job, car, house, neighborhood, income or waist size makes you a good or bad person, then I truly hope, in this time that we've spent together has, at the very least, given you a moment of pause to reconsider that notion. Mind you, I never said that there was anything wrong with money or having nice things. But what I am saying, is that there needs to be an honest understanding that everything else external to you, as in those "things" we pursue so feverishly, really have nothing to do with who we, *you*, really are.

"Okay Chase, you're being repetitive again. We already covered this. You said you were going to talk about how you got free. So, can we get to it?"

I told you that I was going to repeat things. I meant it.

When you get a taste of real freedom, there is something otherworldly that happens. When you get a chance to define for yourself, those things that are who you really are, what you really want, how you really want to live, there is, peace. But what others tend to forget to mention in all of their "self-help" manuals, as we have talked about, is that it will not always be easy. People will still have their opinions. There will still be those that might oppose your right to live as you truly desire *and* deserve. But be willing to see yourself as worthy, and when you do, well….

You get to cry different kinds of tears. Tears that don't start in the pit of your stomach, in some dark and lonely place, but rather, tears that start in the wellspring of love and hope in the heart. I know that it might sound trite, or like I'm full of shit but, that is why I shared my life's experiences with you the way that I did. See, the idea was, is, very simple to me (now):

Most of the things that we have been told about ourselves, by others, that we've sadly bought into, are bullshit. Plain and simple.

When you get on the path to your truest freedom, scary shit isn't as frightening as it once was because somehow, from someplace, without your assistance, or even your awareness, you have hope. And within that hope, you get to look at yourself in the mirror and love, *fucking love* the person looking back at you. As outlandish as that may seem to some, it's true. And yes, it *is* for you. I didn't believe, at one time, that it was for me, but it was. And is.

When you set your heart to the path, you will still have to contend with thoughts that would remind you of the old ways of living, of who you once believed yourself to be. For example, just because you get sober, or drug-free, doesn't mean that you won't think about it any longer. But, like everything else we have shared, I assure you, that you have not only the strength to overcome, but it's been there all the time.

When you get a taste of the freedom you were born to, you will know it. You will know that it's your right. You will just, know. I don't have all of the answers, and frankly, I don't believe anyone can really explain it – but it works. It just does.

When you get a taste of truth, of freedom, you are getting a taste of what it means to love.

You will know it as surely as you know that I am telling you the truth about my life. Did I tell you all of it? Certainly not but, I shared with you key aspects of how and why I believed myself unworthy of love.

But I got a taste of freedom. True freedom.

And now, I share with you, step one. May seem too simple, too silly, too basic. Some may think that it lacks all the fervor that we tend to think that a life-change requires, or that somehow, after all that we've heard from other self-help gurus, that it's going to be a process that's going to require skills that we don't already possess. It can be hard to imagine but, I promise, whatever new challenges you may face don't tend to be as dramatic or as draining as continuing to believe that you're not worth loving. Trust me when I say this; there are no shortcuts and this has to be done.

It took me a long to time to understand that this, the *real truth of it all,* was the key for me. That understanding, that acceptance had to come.

The very first step is….

Be You.

Be You.

There is no magic potion, no overnight "trick" or otherworldly fast-track. There are no special passes or memberships needed. There is no secret handshake or grandiose oath that one needs to take.

It will require you to ask a (the) critical question and then, once that is done, it will require honesty, faith and fortitude. It will take time. It will take patience. It will take forgiveness. It will take you letting go of anything and everything, anyone and everyone that would oppose the whole and free expression of who you really are and what you truly desire to be and to have.

Anything and everything, anyone and everyone that would oppose the whole and free expression of who you really are and what you truly desire to be and to have, must Kick Rocks.

Ask, first. Ask often. Ask whenever it is needed.

What is it that you really, *really* want?

Allow yourself the courage to take off the masks you wear to suit the views of others, as to who they believe you are, or should be. Allow yourself the time to get to know that real you, not the pre-packaged person that you've come to accept. Spend time with the person that you are, the one that whispers to you, in that kind and gentle voice, barely audible above the chaos and confusion that we succumb to in the hopes of being liked by others. Yes, Be You.

Allow yourself the freedom to explore the question of what you really, *really* want and then, allow yourself to answer it.

You get to define it. You get to decide who you are. And remember, be patient with yourself.

Remember in the Preface, I shared that I would tell you what I meant by, Soul-Salsa? Well, here it is. I love the Salsa dance and though I couldn't dance it to save my life if I had to, I do know what it feels like, inside, to hear the music and to watch others perform the dance. But that's not even the whole of it. For me, what the dance really means, what it really refers to, is the way that the dancers move and how those dance moves sometimes seem to reflect the feelings in my soul since I found that I was worthy of loving and being loved. Sometimes the dance moves are hyperkinetic and yet, at the same time, they're precise and fluid, graceful and expressive. And that is how I feel inside most of the time. My point is not to convince you that you have to embrace my notion of the Soul-Salsa. Rather, it is my hope that you will seek out those moments, those actions, those reflections of life that are uplifting to *you, and that reflect your newfound joy in loving and living.*

You get to define whatever it is that sparks your unique and beautiful self. You get to decide who you are, and how you want to express the wondrous reflection of sweet awesomeness that you are. And remember, be patient with yourself as you get more and more comfortable with embracing your truest self. On this path of a newly awakened awareness of who you are, what you deserve for your happiness and peace, some of us are over here, some of us are over there but, in every way, we are all *here*. Some silent. Some vocal. And some, like me, are just outrageously out there, loving you 'cause, as I've been saying, we are *all* fucking amazing! *Amazing!* And keep this truth with you always, *always….*

You are not alone anymore.

I can honestly tell you that I have enjoyed this time that we've spent together. I truly hope that as we close out our time together, that you've found some inspiration to set aside the wrong thinking and thoughts that would otherwise seek to hold you back from living and loving the life that you so richly deserve.

Take with you, the inspiration to look around the world and see in others, those that have committed to living and loving freely, and then choose for yourself, how your life story shall be written. Being you, being free – that is the hope, yes?

I know that it may sound so simple. And as I said in the beginning of this book that you're reading right now, I didn't promise you that I would have all the answers for you on how you can live and love the life that you really want. But I did promise you that I would be transparent and honest, that I wouldn't bullshit you with empty promises or vague quotes and euphemisms. All of this, every word, every example and story, and every fiber of my being was all-in and fully committed to this process with you and I, in hopes that my journey, though not yet complete (I ain't dead yet, ya' know!), might inspire you. Inspire you to, Be You.

Here's a truth that I had been searching for, but unable to find, that others never told me in ways that made sense *to me* or that got to the point in a way that I could get my mind and heart around:

To Be You, to live and love the life that you want to love and live, *you* have to decide, *for you.* You must *actively decide and choose* to be the director, the founder, the creator – the liberator of and in your own life. No one, and I mean no one, other than you, has the power to build and live the life that you truly want to love and live.

Want to dance in the rain in a tutu? Then by all that is right and good in this life, dance without strings. Dance and smile, grin and skip – live it, love it – express your heart and soul in the way that liberates you from the fear that would scream in your mind. Not ready to tango in public yet? Then do it in your mind! Tap your toes to the lovely melody in your heart and soul – *no one* can steal your heart and imagination. No one.

Out of everything that I have shared, I hope that you see how that process, for some of us, is short-circuited by the experiences that we've had and in those that cause us to fear and doubt ourselves. Those of us that know the fear and doubt like you and I, know all too well, what it means to fear. What it means to live and suffer the doubts that inhibit us from loving and living. We've felt fearful that we're not qualified to decide for ourselves how our own life should be and worse still, that if we do decide, that it won't work, or that it will all end up turning to shit. So since that's what we believe, we don't do anything that really sparks our hearts and souls to speak the language of our freedom and passions about the *true* freedom that only comes from loving one's self. We become frozen and stuck. Depressed. But you and I are equipped to change all of that and it's my deepest, and most sincere hope, that this little book of mine will inspire you to take that first step. For you.

For your love. For your life.

There is no one on this planet better-equipped than you are, to determine for you, how you want your life to be. I am not being funny. I am not being cute.

This whole journey that you and I have just shared, has been about inspiration. This life that we've been living and the "secrets" of true happiness, as it were, and the truth is, that I, you, all of us, are *the* secret to the life we desire to love and live. We are, despite what others may have tried to convince us of, is that we are our own "secret"; that through it all, *we* are the beautiful parts, pieces, mysteries and hidden treasures. A part of a wondrously glorious life that we get to share, if we're willing.

I was willing. And if you've gotten this far in our little conversation, well, it means that you were kinda willing too. And hopefully, even more so now.

Finally, dear reader, there is something that I want to leave with you, and I believe that you will understand why, so I won't get into my reasons for asking. But I want to hear from you. I want to know how it all progresses for you. Write to me and share with me your stories, your triumphs. Your hopes. Your dreams.

As I have shared with you, share with me. We are, one.

And remember, I love you.

Now go, Kick Rocks - Be Real. Be Free. Be You.

And if you're wondering, yes, this book and every word, is my written testament that there is hope, faith and life to be lived.

And love abundantly.

So, my dear reader, get your pad and pen and start writing your own love story.

"Love endures with patience and serenity, love is kind and thoughtful...." – Amplified Bible, 1 Corinthians 13:4

Be patient with yourself. Be willing to laugh at the absurdity of trying to be someone else's idea of, "perfect". Your serenity is your right to have and hold but, be patient as you allow yourself to get acquainted with the true you. Be kind and thoughtful to yourself. See yourself through thoughtful, considerate eyes, and with a heart founded in and on forgiveness. Set aside the jealousy that you might have for the "better" person you think that you could, or should, be; they don't exist. The most amazing person you are, is here, *right now*. What happens ten minutes, ten weeks or ten years from now, is a matter of experiences, not of "getting better". There is no "better" you. Love you, right the hell now.

Be thoughtful of and to yourself, and take account of your beautiful soul. Be thoughtful of and to yourself and the dreams you hold, and allow yourself to believe in, you.

Be you, in the moment, in the "now", and today, if you can, step away from everyone else, for just a moment, and smile. Smile because no one can take that away from you. Smile, because in that moment, in that gentle, yet powerful gesture, you are reminding yourself that so long as you have the power to smile, you have the power to live. To truly live.

And remember, each of us, every moment of every day, are writing our own love story.

And you and I, well, we've only just gotten started….

Yours truly,
Chase Murphy, Jr.
chase.murphy@chasemurphyjr.com

Figure 1 - The author at age 13. Lost and confused.

Figure 2 - The author at age 50. Lovin' life!

Be Real. Be Free. Be You.

Be You.

Be You.

Be You.

Be You.

Be You.

Be You.

Be You.

Be You.

Be You.

Be You.

Be You.

A special note, for a very special few of you. We may never get the chance to meet face-to-face but, I hope that you know that there are those of us that have found peace and happiness, that stand ready to support you. Not all are as vocal and as in-your-face as I am but, we are there. We are here. Trust yourself to ask the hard questions of us, and then have the courage to trust what your "gut" tells you. Yes, I know, for many of us, it was our trusting way, our trusting nature that seemed to have been a reason that we suffered through what we did. But you cannot, must not, extinguish the light in you.

We are out here. Willing and able.

And we're not all silent. Find us, keep looking for us because, we're out here.

And a lot of us, well, we're looking for you too.

As I have been saying all throughout this book, if people don't like you just the way you are, they can go fuck themselves sideways. But if you're still not ready to believe that you should like yourself, as this whole book has tried to do, try, right now, if only for a moment, to inspire yourself to listen to your own inner voice. The other one, and you know which one I'm talking about. Yes, the one that is telling you the truth. No, not the bullshit about yourself but, the whole truth, the real truth, the fact:

You are amazing just as you are.

Fucking amazing!

Finally, if you're still wrestling with it, go back and look my pictures. Yes, I know that they're small but, look anyway. At 13, even in a picture, you can see that I was just not happy. Not about a given moment but, my soul was aching. You can see it. It's in the eyes. Then look at 50. Look closely.

If that doesn't inspire you, well....

I didn't just stumble into 50, I found the love – and the courage to write this book!

You. Are. Amazing.

Believe it.

Live it.

www.ingramcontent.com/pod-product-compliance
Lightning Source LLC
Chambersburg PA
CBHW061146040426
42445CB00013B/1573